The masculine gender is used throughout this book for reasons of simplicity and is not meant to be discriminatory. **"MUSHER"** is an asexual title awarded by a pack of sled dogs to their master.

Published by Edition Marquis Ltd
Montmagny (Québec)

Legal deposit third trimester 1999
National Library of Canada
National Library of Québec
ISBN : 2-9800446-5-2

ANDRÉ PILON
coureur de bois

THE UNIVERSE OF SLED DOGS

Willow

MANY THANKS !

I wish to thank those who helped me with the writing of this book. Without them, this entire exercise would have been in vain.

PHOTOGRAPHS

National Library of Canada
Boyer, Bernard
Brault, Lucien
Dupuis, Louis
Royal Canadian Mounted Police
Léger, Patricia
Pilon, André Jr.

SKETCHES

Laberge, Maryse

CONTRIBUTORS

Binette, Yvan
Hart, Claude
Lachance, Monique
Pagé, Marc-Hubert, DVM
Pearce, Bryan, Judith
Pilon, Gérard
Thibert, Danielle-Andrée

REVISION

Brault, Marcelle
Cryer, Donna
Dion, Mireille
Hooker, Rosemary

SECRETARY

Primeau, Sylvianne L.

GRAPHICS

PCG, publicité et conception graphique

TRANSLATORS

Pearce, Bryan
Pearce, Judith

THE UNIVERSE
OF
SLED DOGS

Polar

North Star

Jean Lebel, Québec 1923

Imagine yourself standing on the runners of a dog sled, the master of a team of **six Siberian Huskies running silently through the swirling flakes of a snow storm** along an old trapper's trail. Magic! Be careful! The benevolent mushing virus may be sleeping in you!

The sled dog was an indispensable winter companion to the early voyagers. They were a part of the conquest of both the North and the South poles. Their endurance and their work ethic, as well as their devotion to their masters since the beginning of time made these animals the best friends and companions of the Nordic races. Certainly in today's world, the sled dog, like the horse, has been largely replaced as an aid to transportation by snowmobiles, airplanes, and all terrain vehicles. Still, an outing with a dog team and accoutrements leaves no one indifferent, especially if that person is driving the team. As the "**driver**" or "**musher**", **you know each of your team players intimately**, not only by name, appearance and behavior, but also by each tiny personality trait. About fifteen years ago I had a team of eighteen Samoyeds. This activity at that time was not widely known or appreciated. There were a few scattered demonstrations at winter carnivals, but not much more. People were more occupied with the evolution of our "consumer society". Certainly the last several years have seen a veritable frenzy of consumerism. Sectors of sled dog sports have really only come of age in the last few years. Each weekend, "mushers" or dog drivers have a wide range of possible activities from which to choose. Thirty odd kennel owners offer sled dog trips of several hours to several days. During the winter months, these same people are able to offer this pleasure to the public while providing themselves and their faithful companions a method of earning their livelihood. New trails for this old sport are opening up at an astonishing rate. Perhaps this new infatuation will be the death of the noisy snowmobile! Television has contributed to an increased awareness of this component of peoples' search for more connectedness with their environment and an idealized and more simple life style. Movies such as **Toby McTeague** and **Iron Will** are probably familiar to most of you. How can one resist the attraction of these marvelous creatures? Races such as **the Iditarod**, (more than 1000 miles across the state of Alaska), the **Yukon Quest**, (1000 miles between Whitehorse in the Yukon and Fairbanks in Alaska), **the Alpirod**, (more than 600 miles across the Alps), etc. have equally contributed in bringing this activity of age. In fact, though it may seem strange to the uninitiated, the greatest joy of mushers actually has nothing to do with competition per se. Obviously it is enjoyable to measure your team against others, to win ribbons and trophies. But, this does not compare to the profound satisfaction of the musher in being an integral part of a living team, a team that accepts the musher as "team leader". The principal reward is often an appreciation of the commitment of one of your leaders to the common enterprise, or a fleeting glance of the peaceful countryside. All serious hunters after the hunt will not speak of how many birds they brought home, but rather of the successful working relationship they have with their dogs. Imagine multiplying this by twelve!

Personally, I have not competed nor participated in the **Labrador 400**, neither in any other well known competitions or sled dog expeditions. I don't offer sled dog rides for tourists. I do not have a commercial kennel and I am not involved in associated activities such as training schools, supplying equipment, or selling of dog feed. I don't even consider myself an expert in this sport; rather I see myself as still an amateur even after thirty years of studying dogs. In reality, even as a writer, I consider myself somewhat mediocre;

continually making improvements in order to produce a decent result. Still, there are many reasons that have motivated me to write this book, the most important of which is **my unlimited admiration for working dogs.**

The second reason for writing this book is to make available to the general public the more recent developments in sled dog sports. It is relatively easy to find appropriate documentation, mostly coming out of Alaska, Montana, and Idaho in the United States. However, these books often follow success stories of certain mushers, with limited information of the technical aspects of the sport. If you are reading this, it probably doesn't matter if I am a "big" musher or a "little" one, or if I have won a race or a trophy. More probably, you are searching for information that will allow you to progress in the sport, and to perfect your own techniques.

It is my hope that this book will give an overview of this activity and will help the adept to speed up their integration into the sport. Even experienced mushers will probably find certain information that may help them to improve their techniques. **I wish above all that the information here will help and inspire young people embarking in the world of sled dogs.** This is an invitation to realize your fondest dreams, to be the "leader of the pack". Certainly, if you live on the twenty-first floor of an apartment block in downtown Montréal, I would not recommend that you go out and buy a pack of Malamutes! Sled dogs are creatures that need space and exercise. To keep a husky dog in an apartment might even be considered by some to be a type of physical and mental torture.

I have difficulty understanding why majority of homes in Québec do not have a dog. I feel that I am a bit of a rebel in our civilization of concrete and Nintendo games. This project for me has not been for the writing of the book, nor for the money, nor for the glory. The knowledge that **some people will find the motivation to go outside to enjoy the great outdoors - whether as a spectator, or as an amateur**; it be sufficient to justify my work. Be that as it may, the writing of this book has been a personal incentive to examine in greater detail the many perspectives of this activity. My bonus is that I have been able to perfect my own techniques. I have no regrets. Needless to say, I have gained my experience in dog activities through innumerable lectures and indispensable consultation with specialists in the field. Without this kind of help, it would have been impossible to write anything of merit.

Resist above all the temptation to run out and buy a bunch of dogs, a sled, and other assorted equipment required for this activity. This will not help you to learn the sport. Well before you plunge into this activity, I suggest that you join a club or association of mushers in your region. **Take your time. Go to the club's activities, get to know the people already involved in the sport.** Work with a musher for at least one season before you set out on your own. There will not be a cost for this service; all mushers are more than happy to have someone around willing to help with the many associated tasks. This approach is indispensable as a learning tool. Also, before you are able to train a dog, you must at be least minimally schooled yourself.

To be sure, you will meet some mushers who are reticent to "give away their trade secrets". Don't believe that this approach is the norm. More than likely those mushers are worried that you will find out how little they really know! The twentieth century is the century of communication. The old adage is fully applicable. **"That which one knows thoroughly will be clearly set forth, and the words to express this will arrive spontaneously."**

I have a number of faults, which have contributed to the production of this book. I am espacially curious, headstrong, and always on the look-out for new ideas and techniques. I also believe that it is not necessary to re-invent the wheel. I have visited at least one hundred kennels, read nearly everything that is currently written on the subject of working dogs, and have consulted with resource people whom I have had the good fortune to meet. It has been rare that **a new experience or a new contact in the mushing world has not given me yet another good idea**. I have asked so many questions, not only of the persons that I have met, but also of myself, that it has been impossible not to learn something. It is this wisdom that I have learned that I would like to share with you. I have spent my life with working dogs. Sled dogs have presented yet another view. Learning the management of this group was at times, an exercise in frustration. One of the goals of this book is to help you avoid the errors that I have made.

Why where my dogs able to get loose from their picket lines so often? Because I did not know how to attach them properly. **Why did I have so much difficulty in feeding my dogs, with the bowls, with the building of individual dog houses?** Simply because I did not know about the many details that others had found by experience to be solutions to these problems. **How many times did I think to innovate?** Months later, or even years later, I would meet an old time musher who solved my problem immediately with yet another novel idea. In the following pages, I will attempt to be as precise as possible in the hopes that I will be able to save the newcomer to the sport both time and money. We are living in the twentieth century, the century of communication. A good idea should be able to make its way around the world in a few months. My education is in engineering. Don't expect this book to be a history of my adventures. It could be more aptly described as follows: **"mix a bit of insecticide with baby oil and dab it on your dog's ears to help deter flies from biting them".** If you also have a good idea, I encourage you to inform me. I contribute regularly to a number of publications... and magazines and also appear on many television programs. In this way, I will continue to pass on good ideas. Even if it seems out of context, I invite you now to have a look at the Lexicon at the end of the book. Before beginning our journey through the world of sled dogs, we must be able to speak the same language.

The musher's position of **"team leader"** or **"leader of the pack"** will evolve through sheer determination, work and perseverance. The development of a reasonable team will take several years. The ability to perfect a team into a "well oiled machine" will take a lifetime. Don't forget above all, that your degree of satisfaction will exactly correspond to your involvement with your dogs and nothing else. Above all, don't forget the title **"musher"** is not awarded by a university. It is your dogs that will allow you to assume that honour. But, be careful! Sled dogs are a **highly addictive drug**, which may result not only in an **addiction**, but also in a **dangerous dependence**. The number of dogs generally increases in direct ratio to the degree of intoxication.

Good luck !

HISTORICAL OVERVIEW

mushroomed in the 1970s as a
construction base of the trans-Alaska pipeline. Nearby
military installations and the nation's northernmost
university broaden its growing base.

on the Alaska Railroa
w a center for Alask
e farming region.

s as a camp an
d crews. Bloss
construction d
ield. Nearby p
as an interna
expansion. Rec
thquake and g
er port.

The Army built this ic
1940s as a railway te
personnel to interi
but also relies

Coal mining supported the original
settlement, which was established
in the late 1800s. Later relocated,
the town is now a commercial
fishing port and tourist center.

Established as Fort St.
in 1791. Became a U.
Orthodox church now co

Founded by Aleksandr Baranov in 1792, replacing nearby

*Col. Ramsey team, 3RD all Alaska Sweeptakes
winner Musher John Johnson, 1910*

The dog surely has to have been one of the first animals domesticated by man. Prehistoric man hunted in groups, much the same as a wolf pack does. It is probable that having captured some young wolves, early man trained them to assist in their search for food, thereby benefiting from this natural instinct to hunt. Over the course of centuries, the relationship between man and dog continued to evolve so that today the dog is fondly known as "man's best friend". At the time of the arrival of the Europeans to North America, the aboriginal peoples (Indians and Inuit) were using dogs as beasts of burden to aid in a multitude of daily tasks as well as transporting their belongings from place to place. The Inuit were primarily responsible for developing the concept of using dogs to pull sleds, similar to the activity that we know today. These sled dogs were indispensable to their nomadic lifestyle.

European settlers, following the lead of local Indian tribes, began using dogs for a variety of tasks, including hauling milk, wood, hay, water, bread, ice, maple sap, providing taxi services, and even being involved in transporting arms in some of the war efforts. As soon as in 1668, Courcelles used them to transport army food and ammunitions from Québec to Albany (U.S.A.). In 1675, dog teams where used to carry bricks cooked in Sillery, to Québec City. By the middle of the seventeenth century, dogs were known as "THE HORSES OF THE POOR", for it was only upper class citizens and army generals who had the luxury of owning horses.

In 1822, **Parry** used dogs to transport supplies between boats. In 1850, **McClintock** left with twelve dogs in search of **Sir John Franklin** and covered the 750 kilometer distance at an average of 50 kilometers per day. It wasn't, however, until 1859 when **McClintock's** dogs discovered the remainder of the

17

HISTORICAL OVERVIEW

Franklin expedition, that sled dogs became the norm in polar expeditions. It was one of the sled dog teams of **Frederick Cook** who were the first to arrive at the North Pole on the 21st of April in 1908. It was also by sled dog teams that **Amundsen** succeeded in being the first to reach the South Pole in December of 1911. Captain **Scott** and his men paid with their lives for their lack of confidence in sled dogs on their return trip from the South Pole. It was then that the practice of leaving on expeditions with a hundred or so dogs became more common. As the expedition progressed, weaker animals were slaughtered and used as food for the others.

In Canada, the "**coureurs de bois**" travelled in the summer by canoe, but after freeze-up and the onset of winter, they too used sled dogs in their travels and in their quest for furs. From the middle of the 1700's up to even the 1940's, the use of sled dogs guaranteed mail delivery to more northern villages during the long winter season. Sled dogs also were used to haul goods between settlements, to help in the moving of people from village to village, and even in agricultural pursuits by pulling ploughs to till the soil. In the bigger towns and cities, dogs were used in many ways. The dairies, shop keepers and delivery people happily took advantage of the ease with which these dogs were trained to

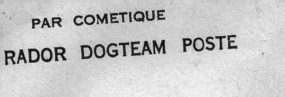

PAR COMETIQUE

RADOR DOGTEAM POSTE

NADIAN DOGTEAM MAIL

_____

QUEBEC

Ralph D...
Whiteville...
U. S. R...

HAVRE ST PIERRE
MR 20
45
P. Q.

PAR COMETIQU...
LABRADOR DOGTEAM M...

Par Cométique
By Labrador Dog-team Post.

QUEBEC
JAN 23
30
P. Q.

CANADA
2 CENTS

NOT CALLED FOR

S. Tanner Green, Esq.,
Mutton Bay,
Co. Charl.-Sag.

Please return
address on...

pull and to work. When they were not working, how-ever, the majority were left loose to roam. This in turn created serious problems of overpopulation, dog bites and attacks, and even wanton killing of livestock. **On the 10th of December 1852, owing to strong public pressure, Québec passed laws prohibiting the use of dogs as draft animals.** Those who did not comply faced a fine of $25.00. This law remained in force for the next seventy years. In 1922, this law was modified. Dog teams were again permitted, but only for public demonstrations, parades or sporting events. Each team required a two dollar permit and the activity itself had to be sanctioned by the Chief of Police and the Animal Protection Society.

In 1904, the missionary ARSEN TURQUETIL used a sled dog team to evangelise the PALDERMIUT. In 1910, he continued his missionary work at Churchill Falls, Chesterfield Inlet, Eskimo Point, Repulse Bay, and Southampton . Most of the early prospectors used sled dogs in their quest for valuable ores. Slowly, but surely, sled dogs began to creep back into people's lives. Added to their function was the transportation of the mail, particularly along the north shore of the St-

Klondike card game, 1897

Lawrence river as far as Blanc Sablon. Gradually horses and snowmobiles assumed most of the dogs' work, except for the mail which was still delivered by dog teams as late as 1950 in Northern villages.

During **the gold rush at the turn of the century**, roads into the Yukon and Alaska did not exist. Sled dogs met this challenge and became indispensable in transporting vital supplies to the gold miners during the long winter months. The majority of these dog teams were driven by French-Canadians who had previously been engaged in driving dog teams for the fur trade. Already skilled in surviving in northern climates and in working with these animals, these mushers adapted quickly and with ease to their new jobs.

The most popular size of working dog was seventy-seven to one hundred and twenty pounds. Their work included pulling heavy loads over particularly difficult and accident prone terrain. Even the **Royal Canadian Mounted Police** used sled dogs until 1969 for their patrols of the enormous wild territories of the Yukon and the North West Territories where few or no roads existed. Dog drivers used the command **"marche"** to have their teams begin or to pull with greater force. They, themselves, were often called **"marcheurs"**. Today the word "marcheurs" is not used. Instead the anglicized version **"musher"** is the term to describe someone who drives a dog team.

At the turn of the century, the Canadian Government, worried about maintaining Canadian sovereignty over the Yukon and North West Territories, sent the RCMP to patrol these Arctic regions. During the summer, all of these patrols were accomplished on foot or by canoe via the many waterways. Alternately, in the winter, sled dogs took over this task. **Constable Harry Mapley** ran the first patrol between Dawson and Fort

21

R.C.M.P. visiting St-Roch at Tree River, N.W.T. 1931

R.C.M.P. visiting a trapper, Forth Smith, N.W.T. 1959

McPherson during the **winter of 1904-1905.** This patrol was comprised of five dog teams of five dogs each, five mushers, and two native guides. This was a two month trek. On their return, the patrol leader suggested that in the future, two more persons on snowshoes should be added to the group with their sole task being that of breaking trail. This they felt would speed up their journeys by allowing the dog teams to move on at a more brisk pace.

In 1911, **Inspector Francis Joseph Fitzgerald** of the **RCMP** and three of his men perished after having been lost on the **Wind River of the Yukon between Fort McPherson and Dawson City.** In their desperate efforts to survive, dogs were slaughtered one by one to be used as food for the remaining dogs and men.

With temperatures in the minus fifty degrees Fahrenheit range, these men died less than fifty kilometers from Fort McPherson. They had followed the small **Wind River** after having lost their way at **Forest Creek.** Bad temperature, coupled with lack of provisions, contributed to their demise. These men had worn the best clothing available for northern climates: woolen underwear, double parkas lined with fur, and moccasins and mukluks on their feet. They had down-filled sleeping bags, a trapper's stove, a tent, tarps and three dog sleds, ten feet long.

The sleds had been loaded with provisions for thirty days, including amongst other things, nine hundred pounds of dried fish for the dogs, eighteen pounds of candles, twenty pounds of tobacco and other assorted supplies for a total weight of thirteen hundred pounds. In addition, each sled had a rifle, an axe and various camping articles bringing the total sled weight up to three thousand pounds. The men's food included seventy-five pounds of bacon, twelve pounds of salted beef, salt, sugar, butter, flour, dried fruits, pork and beans, coffee, tea, baking powder, etc. These provisions proved to be insufficient to accommodate the men when an additional forty miles of travel was added by going in the wrong direction.

The Inspector had kept a daily journal describing their experiences. The search team sent out to find them found this journal along with the bodies of the expired men. It described in detail their search for **Forest Creek**, and then their loss of hope as they were forced to sacrifice the dogs one by one for food. Why did this patrol lose its way? Why did they not realize their route error and turn around earlier? Why was the native guide **Gwich** not with them? These are questions that remain unanswered nearly a century later. In the years that followed, shelters were erected at strategic locations and stocked with food. Trails were marked with greater care. The RCMP continued its dog team patrols of the Yukon for an additional twenty years without another such incident. A silver dollar coin was struck in commemoration of the last dog team patrol of the history of the RCMP.

By the 1950's, the glimmer of competition was in place. Teams consisted of the dogs, one driver, and one person on snowshoes to break the trail. The Stadacona Sled Dog Club was founded with about six members. This club managed the Québec City sled dog race as an integral part of the winter "CARNAVAL DE QUÉBEC". In 1970, the Stadacona Sled Dog Club became incorporated under the name of the "Club d'Attelages des Chiens de Québec". The CACQ is still flourishing, providing guidance, education, good races, and competitive mushers in the speed sector of the sport. There are now more than 800 dogs mushers in the province of Québec, which represent around 10,000 northern breed dogs.

Inuit sleds

Overnight camping
March 15, 1820

More and more concerned individuals are becoming involved with groups associated with animal protection. One might even say that it has become fashionable to join one of these associations. Certainly it does not require a high degree of commitment to send some money in response to carefully chosen pictures suggesting animal abuse. **This, however, makes the individual feel better, as though he is contributing to the eradication of something bad. An easy mission!**

Pets make up a sector of society that is probably the most poorly managed, not only in Canada, but also elsewhere in the world. What is the population of cats and dogs in Québec? Very difficult to evaluate. What percentage of these dogs and cats receive the minimal medical care of deworming, vaccinations, etc.? This is even more difficult to evaluate. Probably the percentage is very low. The fact that few statistics are available gives one food for thought. The SPCA of Montréal euthanizes thousands of dogs and cats. How many others in the private clinic sector add to the euthanasia numbers of the SPCA? We don't know, but the numbers are certainly significant.

The care and feeding of sled dogs is essential to the animals' ability to accomplish their function as a worker, regardless of other reasons. **This alone dictates that sled dogs probably have better overall health and care than the average pet.**

Seal hunters on the Magdalen Islands believed in the concept of non-cruelty to animals and felt that they conducted their hunts with this in mind. When they were approached by Animal Rights groups, invitations were issued to observe the hunt. Several years later, these extremists had effectively reduced the seal hunters' livelihood to a subsistence level. Even international inquiries, which had pronounced themselves in favour of the basic concept of the seal hunt, were unable to change the demise of this activity. The same type of experience has also occurred within the trapping community. Valid criticism of the cruelty of certain traps led to the development of the "quick kill" trap. But this was not enough for those more enlightened. Gradually, the market demand for furs was also reduced by significant percentage.

There is no reason for mushers to resign themselves to the same eventual fate. It is not possible to reason with these extremists and their narrow-minded and simplistic approach.

Tolerance is the virtue of virtues. The great majority of sled dogs are vaccinated, and receive only state of the art veterinary health care. Their excellent physical condition and health is in sharp contrast to the multiple health problems presented by the average pet dog. And finally, the issue of psychological problems presented by apartment living animals is only now beginning to be addressed.

Although it is rare, there are on occasion those mushers who become angry at their dogs. Neither can we hide the fact that some dogs die each year in the competitive sector of the sled dog sports. In the human world, there are parallels. The champion skater Gerguei Grinkov died from cardiac problems at the age of twenty-eight. **Sled dogs, too, are athletes working at a very intense level of activity**. Therefore it is not surprising that there are some injuries and some fatalities. If you were a dog, **wouldn't you prefer to be on the trail going somewhere with the rest of your buddies than being required to lie quietly on the living room rug twenty-four hours a day with little reprieve?**

THE DOGS

Maple sugar time

Taking a walk

Introduction

In comparison to other modes of transportation, the sled dog offers some absolutely matchless advantages. It is fueled by energy sources both renewable and diversified. It starts immediately, even in sub-zero temperatures, and is able to traverse any terrain, including stretches of water. It possesses its own repair system, creates its own future models and replacements through reproduction, has a built-in alarm system and even supplies evening concerts for free. Its greatest quality, however, which no other manufacturer has been able to build into its machines, **is its very presence, is that of a friend**.

Your choice of a dog will doubtless be the most important decision you will have to make. This decision will have direct consequences on your future activities. Each breed of dog has its own natural aptitudes and qualities, both physical and psychological, which you must evaluate. It is impossible to make a **Basset Hound** or a **Saint Bernard** into a pointer in order to hunt woodcocks. This dimension is not as evident for sled dogs. The great majority of dogs, whatever their ancestors, love to run and I think that most would be able to be trained to pull a sled. However, there are basic considerations that deserve your attention and consideration. These animals will have to work during winter. You must choose a breed which tolerates snow and cold weather. Given that these animals will have to pull heavy loads, they must also have a physical structure which will permit them to apply reasonable power to the task. These are working dogs. They must possess the necessary endurance for the type of activity you intend to pursue. According to what you expect to do with your dogs, choose the type of dog which best suits your needs. If you want to pull heavy loads, some distance at reasonable speeds, think of a **Alaskan**

ALL ABOUT THE DOGS

Introduction

Malamute or similar size dogs. If you want to make trips at somewhat higher speeds and longer distances, the **Siberian Husky** or **Samoyed** would be your choice. If you want to win races, consider an **Alaskan husky**. Of course, you can make a sled dog out of a **Labrador Retriever**, a **pointer** or a **black and tan hound**, but it takes time and it would be surprising if you were satisfied with the results.

One of the essential qualities of a sled dog is **stamina** or **endurance**, that is, his capacity to produce a strong effort (cardio-vascular) over a long period of time (aerobic cycle). The second quality, equally indispensable, is the willingness of your team to work together with you. The first quality is an issue of genetics and natural physiology. Certainly, good nutrition and good health care help in the development of the dog's capacity to run long distances. The second, **the degree of collaboration with the musher** and the other dogs in the team, will depend to a large degree on their training.

Contrary to companion dogs, your dogs must not systematically seek your presence nor should they display the characteristic independence of cats, but rather want to become part of your team. They must not fear you, but respect you. I have had the opportunity to train Samoyeds, Alaskans, Siberian Huskies and Malamutes. Running in harness is almost automatic. Some that you slip a harness on and hook in with an experienced team, take only a minute to learn what took me years to show my Saint Bernards. Certainly there exist other qualities nearly as important. Sled dogs are called upon to mingle with the public, with other dogs, and most significantly, are often in contact with children. **It is essential that they be sociable**. It is necessary

Introduction

that as early as a few weeks old, puppies are put into contact with people, dogs and a variety of situations, in order that they develop a high level of socialization. One must be careful of dogs raised in large kennels, in a pack, without other social contacts than their owners.

Even though appearance would not be a criteria of excellence, I give it high importance. It is this factor, similarly, which develops the uniformity of your team. It is almost impossible to develop a well performing team with dogs of different sizes or different temperaments. I have seen too often a collection of Samoyeds, Malamutes and pointers, which individually would have given good results, but, when placed in the same team were completely inefficient.

Animals of a registered breed generally give results which are consistent with their genetic type. However, constant breeding within a limited group (without proper diversity) produces more unhealthy animals. The non-registered crosses, such as the Alaskan huskies, produce a range of descendants according to their ancestors. The best ones generally come from crosses between ancestors of superior quality. But, it is necessary to pay great attention before beginning this type of experimentation. The owner of one kennel, of international calibre, told me that he kept only one out of a hundred pups. When you buy a dog of a registered breed, you have the likelihood of gaining the qualities of this breed. When you buy a dog from a serious breeder of sled dogs, there is a good chance that your puppy will become a very good sled dog. If, however, you take your chance with cross breeds, you are playing russian roulette and your chances of finding one for your benefit are significantly less.

ALL ABOUT THE DOGS

Introduction

Above all, at the beginning, do not consider becoming a breeder. This decision requires knowledge as well as adequate kennel arrangements. By visiting and talking with mushers from your region, I am certain that you will be able to make a better decision. Certainly, do not skimp on the price of your future companions.

A dog is a long term investment. In all ways, imagine the money you will save. While you will be training your dogs you will not have the time to go to the local tavern, nor the time to go skiing, still less to fool around with electronic games. Think twice before getting a bigger team. Three dogs are manageable; you can have a lot of fun with a team as pets. It can also get very expensive. Many people have found themselves in over their heads. Most cities allow a maximum of 2 or 3 dogs per house. Your dogs can be shared with an other musher in order to form a bigger team to hitch to a regular sled.

It is important that you understand from the beginning that your new companions are living beings; that all living beings, even similar in breed, age and sex, are different individuals. **Each has his own temperament, behaviour, qualities and faults**. Understand quickly that the one you intend to lead your team will often reveal himself to be quite ordinary and that the one whose appearance seems to assign him to a secondary role may become your leader.

I am often surprised that many visitors think that I do not know the names of each one of my dogs. I consider this to be an insult. **All mushers know not only the name of each of their dogs, but also their temperament, strengths and weaknesses.** A musher

Introduction

can recognize each of his dogs even in the dark of night by his pulling style, his running and even his way of sleeping. You need only to observe a musher speaking to each of his dogs before starting, to understand that a dog team, above all, is a team made up of individuals, each having its own characteristics. Since you are putting together a group of living beings, each with its own mood, desires, qualities and faults, success will depend on bringing about a sense of collaboration among the members of this team. Otherwise, the results will be disappointing. Your team will be what you will have made it, nothing more, nothing less.

A good musher must be, at times, a **veterinarian, a nutritionist, a psychologist, an engineer, and above all, a resourceful person**. He must also possess good physical endurance, and a practical knowledge of the winter environment. If you believe it is enough to buy four adult dogs from a qualified breeder to become a musher, you are greatly deceiving yourself. It is far from certain that these dogs will accept you as the master of the team. One question is often put to me. Must a dog always be tied or caged to maintain its **will to pull** ? The answer is simple, and unequivocal : NO.

In fact, most lead dogs receive special attention from their musher, and this is important. If you wish to improve communication with your dog, you must increase your time with him. You have certainly noticed that most sled dogs have a strong habit of running around the post or in the pen. This is one of the contributing factors in their physical condition. It is clear that if you keep your dog in an apartment, or he spends the day in your truck, he will have difficulty keeping up the same rhythm as the other better conditioned members of the team.

ALL ABOUT THE DOGS

Introduction

In every situation, whatever activity you plan for your dog, he must be socialized. This involves feeding him, petting him and committing some time each day to him. It is equally important that your dogs be not fearful of strangers, neither people nor other dogs. Never miss an opportunity to have a visitor pet your dog. Even then, certain dogs develop strange behaviour with women or children. Male dogs not raised among females in season are more excited when they encounter such a situation than males raised in larger kennels where there is regular exposure to the odour of females in season.

Anik & Yukon - André Jr. & Montana

Introduction

If you see a group of sled dogs, in pens or attached to posts, you will note that unlike other breeds, **these dogs seem to be always in motion**. They pace, jump up and down from their houses and run in circles with no apparent reason. If you approach them, most of these dogs, instead of coming to meet you, run even faster, as if they wish to show you their love of running.

When a musher enters his kennel to choose those to go on the next run, you will notice that no force is required: **each dog wants to have a harness put on.** Watch the reaction of a husky when the musher shows him a harness. He throws himself into it with enthusiasm, raising each foot to help the musher put the harness on. The disappointment of the dogs not chosen for this run is clear.

Watch how impatient the dogs are, straining to pull the sled, even as the musher tries to call them. Their instinct to run and to pull is impossible to contain. When a dog finds himself accidentally loose before the team has left, most of the time he will run some distance, only to return to the musher and team when he realizes he is alone.

If, for whatever reason, you need to take a dog out of the team, what do you do? Simply let the dog loose (except in competition, or if the dog is hurt) and do you know what happens? This dog will continue to run behind the sled, and after a few minutes, most likely he will return and simply run in his place in the team. The musher will simply stop the team and reattach the dog, then continue the run.

These animals love to run, love to pull the sled, love the pack and only need a musher to bring

it together. Even if equipment breaks, it is rare that the musher loses the team. In most instances, some of the dogs notice the absence of the musher; they stop, as if helpless, and await their leader.

What is more depressing for a living being than to have nothing to do? **Most sled dogs (Samoyeds, Siberian Huskies, Alaskan Malamutes and Alaskan Racing Huskies) are pack animals.** These dogs don't tolerate inactivity, isolation or overcrowding. They are not apartment dogs. Their life is the outdoors and running. These dogs want so much to run that the musher must constantly use his judgement, not to encourage them to run, but most of the time to slow them down, even stop them, to avoid exhaustion.

What do you think a musher gives his dogs for food? I have been to hundreds of kennels, learning that the dogs usually eat better than their musher. And it is the same for all of their care. It is easy to guess the living standard of a musher. Look at his kennel and divide by two. He spends about twice the average than he allows himself on his dogs. I gave up a long time ago trying to convince the Nintendo generation that their physical activities limit them to searching in a bag of chips and unscrewing a Pepsi. **Participaction** tried, unsuccessfully, for 20 years to get this generation to take up outdoor activities.

I think we must direct our efforts towards educating our young people, who are more open, more willing to discover the virtues of work, of physical exercise, of the need to excel. Initiating a young person to this sport would have an irreversible effect on his philosophy regarding the relationship between humans and animals. It seems to me essential that the young be able

Introduction

to make a distinction between a **wild animal (e.g. a wolf), a working dog (e.g. a Husky) and a pet dog (e.g. a Poodle)**.

I have been very surprised at the number of retired people who decided to move and spend their latter years in the North. In most instances you would see a dozen huskies behind their cabin. Actually, my greatest surprise has been to realize that most of these people were professionals who had spent their life at the centre of large American and Canadian cities, people whom I had considered beyond hope. Personally, I have introduced hundreds of young people to survival techniques in the woods, to fishing, to hunting and to trapping fur-bearing animals, and to using sled dogs. In each session I was able to see their enthusiasm, their intelligent questions, and their judgement, so much more accurate than that of their parents.

I am optimistic by nature, I have helped to reverse the demise of the fur market. I am seeing now the population explosion of sled dogs. Obviously, this is probably a passing fad because one must be realistic. This marvellous sport is reserved for a minority who not only must have the means to care for at least four dogs, but who can provide the space and time to run them. To those of you who are unable to afford such an extravagance, I suggest you pay for the experience of driving a team from time to time.

There are three main categories where one can enjoy sled dogs: **pleasure outings, racing in competitions and expeditions.**

Nome, Alaska, 1996

Activities

ENJOYING YOUR DOG TEAM

More and more dog owners, of all breeds, have a sled or an A.T.V. allowing them to hook up their dogs. The equipment is often very different, and the dogs performance varies greatly. What is important is neither the speed, nor the distance, but rather **the relationship between the musher and his dogs, in this mosquito free world.**

This, without any doubt, is the ideal way to start in the sport. It allows you at the same time to initiate your family to the sport. If you go to the trails, you will be surprised at the number of women who are driving dog teams.

Anouk, Trapper, Arctic, Zamouray, Taku, Monique and Gérard
Les Forestiers, St-Lazare, 1996

ALL ABOUT THE DOGS

RACES

The dogs used in racing are usually well matched. They are, in fact, athletes. To achieve significant results, the musher must commit many hours of training and use specially designed diets. Even if one speaks of the dedication of all people working with dogs, racing sled dogs represents an activity which regularly takes all the free time of the musher. **It is an extremely demanding and costly venture almost in the same realm as an addiction to drugs.** Each weekend there are many races one might choose to enter. Maybe, one day, this sport will be known as an Olympic event. It was a demonstration sport at the 1932 Lake Placid Winter Olympics, and was presented in conjunction with the Winter Olympics at Calgary and Albertville in France.

1. Kojak 2. Red 3. Yumak 4. Isdra 5. Kairos 6. Chester 7. Jasper
Bryan Pearce, Kirkland, 1978

Activities

EXPEDITIONS

The dogs used for this type of work are usually more muscular and show a clearer relationship with the musher, the head of the team. Whether this trip be a long expedition, for giving rides to clients, for a rescue mission, or to work a trapline, these working dogs must possess endurance, patience, physical strength and, above all, a remarkable spirit of team work. Moving on little maintained trails for long hours and camping in the middle of nature, etc. reinforces and strengthens the team spirit not only among the dogs but also with their musher. **No dog driver is able to claim the title 'musher' who has not slept in the woods with his dogs, or camped on a lake and fished in order to feed his faithful companions.**

All mushers dream of the great long distance races (The Iditarod, The Yukon Quest, The Labrador 400). These races demand incredibly detailed planning. The dogs must be trained over a long period of time. Then, each detail (food, equipment, route) must be carefully studied.

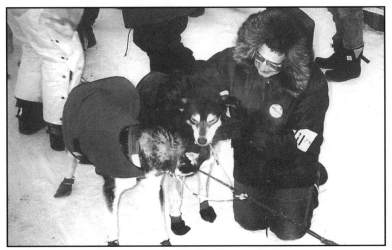

Jenny Stewart
Nome, Alaska 1995

Alaskan

Akita

Samoyed

Groenland

Siberian Huskies

Breeds

Northern peoples, for thousands of years, have raised sled dogs to assist them in surviving their rather difficult environment. In time, certain groups developed their own breeds, which now carry their names. In this way the **white Samoyed**, which was so popular with some of the first explorers of both the Arctic and the Antarctic, was developed by the 'Samoyede' people who lived in the east-central part of Siberia. **Malamutes**, developed by the Inuit of the northwest of Alaska (Malemuit) served to haul heavy sleds over long distances. The **Siberian Husky** was brought to North America at the beginning of the 20th century specifically to race in the **All Alaska Sweepstakes** and this breed was so good that the majority of sled dogs actually have some percentage of siberian blood in them. The **Alaskan husky** is a mix of many breeds, including wolf, in order to increase what is commonly called **'stamina'** or endurance. Certainly if one wants only speed, **hounds** would not have any serious opponents. However, given that sled dogs must have many other characteristics, such as endurance, power, resistance to the cold, efficient metabolization of food, it is rare that one sees many non-nordic breeds being used as sled dogs. Racers, all the same, have "cross bred" with some success, fast dogs with Siberian huskies or Malamutes. Hunting dogs (pointers, retrievers, sight hounds) have been used successfully, particularly in Alaska. One might even see an Irish Setter leading a team of huskies. However, the organizers of the major races have made regulations to avoid allowing dogs who are not northern breeds, and who may not be able to tolerate climactic conditions, to participate.

It is a shame that the Alaskan husky has not been recognized by the Canadian Kennel Club. These dogs have been developed specifically for sledding by the specialists in this field. The true Alaskan is the result of crosses between the best individual dogs who have won races or completed long expeditions. The absence of rules prevents the registration of pedigrees. Nonetheless, these animals are likely more efficient than the registered breeds. This is a problem which breeders, sooner or later must face. Today, buying an Alaskan cannot be done other than on the good faith and reputation of the breeder. **If your goal is to win races, the Alaskan will be your only choice.** A breeder convinced me that other breeds required twice as much training to reach the same conditioning level of an Alaskan. The true Alaskans now represent more stable standards for conformation, probably superior to the recognized breeds which have evolved in two contexts, show and working.

Crosses between shorthaired pointers and greyhounds are now very popular in Europe for short and mid-distance races. Some experts say these crosses are only fads or experiments. However, it must be said that **the winning teams in Sweden and Norway are often composed of dogs which are 7/8 Northern breeds and 1/8 Shorthaired pointers**.

Unless you have many years of experience in this field, and have available excellent, proven breeding stock, I do not encourage you to risk these experiments. You are simply playing Russian roulette and your chances of success are minimal.

IDENTIFICATION

If your dogs are purebred and you want to register them in the Canadian Kennel Club, you must identify each of your dogs. Two methods may be used -

Breeds

the first being a tatoo of the animal's registration identification number on the inside of the flank, on the stomach or in the ear, and the second, the insertion of an electronic microchip under the skin. However, even if you are not required to identify your dogs, it is strongly recommended that you do so. This identification will be very useful if you happen to lose your dog. It would be easy for whoever finds the dog to identify him.

The Canadian Kennel Club recommends a microchip. It is simply an **electronic emitter the size of a grain of rice** and is enclosed in a bio-medically safe capsule. Each emitter has a letter and number code, allowing each animal to have its own distinct identification number. Each microchip is inserted with a sterilized disposable needle. It is put under the skin between the shoulder blades along the spinal column. The microchip is an inert passive element, and is inactive until it is scanned. **The identification number in the microchip appears on the screen when scanned**.

This method has several advantages.

* The insertion of a microchip assures the permanent, direct and unique identification of an animal for its whole life.

* Microchips used as a method of identification are not able to be altered and do not degenerate over time.

* This method is simple, safe and painless. It requires neither anesthetic nor a surgical procedure.

* Most protection societies, veterinarians and animal shelters have, or will soon have, the equipment necessary to read microchips, since the scanners are given to

them without charge. Canada Chip (1-800-396-1896) can immediately give the necessary information to bring about the safe return, of the animal to its owner. Up to now, more than 2,000 dogs and cats carrying microchips have been found in Canada.

IMPLANTATION

The microchip is shipped in a sterile package. It comes with the necessary implantation equipment. Four labels of bar codes are attached to the back of the sterile package. A copy of this label must be attached to each of 3 copies of the registration form supplied by Canada Chip. The last one may be put in the dog owner's file.

The registration form must be fully completed and the white copy sent to Canada Chip so that the information can be put into the central file as soon as possible. The second copy is given to the client and the third copy is kept by the veterinarian clinic or hospital.

This form is not a substitute for CKC individual dog registration. Purebred dogs must be registered with CKC using valid registration forms and procedures.

The injectable emitter is an extremely reliable mechanism, with a useful life expectancy of 25 years. The implant includes an anti-migratory tip which keeps the microchip under the skin between the shoulder blades and prevents it from moving. The microchip has been used in many experiments in universities and scientific laboratories on animal species as small as birds, mice and even salmon. When the microchip has been correctly placed, it does not leave a mark any

Breeds

more obvious than any other injection or innoculation. The entry site will heal quickly and the wound will eventually disappear.

The microchip is placed in a waterproof, biocompatible material. The manufacturer's studies reveal that the mechanism, once in place, causes minimal inflammation and 'minimal tissue reaction'. Given that the microchip is implanted under the skin of the animal, the animal develops a thin layer of protective tissue around the mechanism, leaving it practically imperceptible to touch only a few days after insertion. The minimal cost of this type of identification is affordable to all serious breeders. Moreover, it is more discreet and, above all, more easily interpreted than tatoos or ear marks. I think that some time from now this system will allow a better control of all dogs.

For more information, you can contact the Canadian Kennel Club, Commerce Park, 89 Skyway Avenue, Suite 100, Etobicoke, Ontario, M9W 6R4, tel : 416-675-5511; web site : www.ckc.ca

The microchip is shipped in a sterile package.

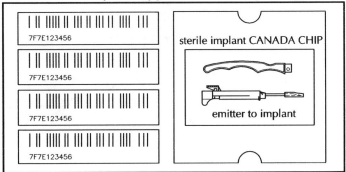

STERILE IMPLANT AND BAR CODES

Breeds

choice for implant site

With the thumb and index finger, raise the skin at the injection site. While holding the handle of the injector in the manner shown in the illustration, insert the needle sub-cutaneously in the region under your thumb. The needle must be inserted completely.

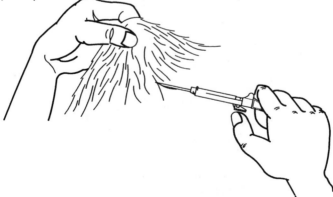

Toundra's basket of joy

Choosing a dog

The purchase of a dog is almost always a gamble when the results will not be known until several years later. Whether it is a puppy or an adult, your first decision will be to choose a breeder. **Remember that you are looking for a dog to pull a sled, and not to enter dog shows.** Regardless of the size of the kennel, the breeds available or the number of animals, look for the following qualities:

* The seller must have an excellent and honest reputation. Don't hesitate to obtain references from other buyers and verify that they are happy with their purchases. Don't buy on your first visit. Take some time to reflect.

* His kennel must be clean and well laid out, demonstrating that the animals there receive adequate care.

* It is important to ask the breeder the nature of the guarantee he offers. In the case of an adult dog, is he able to show the dog in action? Will you be allowed to try the dog for a couple of weeks?

If this is possible, bring with you an experienced musher who has no other interest in the transaction.

After having chosen the kennel you want to deal with, there remains the choice of the dog or dogs and this isn't easy.

Ask all the questions you want, however, don't forget these :

Choosing a dog

FOR THE PURCHASE OF A PUPPY

Age, sex, general appearance ?
Number and sex of the puppies in the litter ?
Worming program ?
Vaccination certificate ?
What is the puppy's behaviour among other dogs ? Is it hyperactive, aggressive, sociable ?
What does he eat ? Does he drink well ?
Does he have a good build compared to the others in the litter ?
Know his pedigree for at least three generations. Can you see his parents ? Are they registered ? Can the puppies be registered ?
Examine the dog to discover physical anomalies, injuries, coat problems, problems with the feet, etc.
Is the seller keeping some puppies of the litter ? Will you have the first choice ?
What is the puppy's weight and how much will he be expected to weigh as an adult ?
Is he appropriate for the type of activities you plan to do ?
Are his parents shy, aggressive, sociable ?

Choosing a dog

FOR THE PURCHASE OF AN ADULT

How old is he ? If he is less than two years old, ask these same questions of his parents.
Why is the dog being sold ?
Where has the dog been hooked into the team ? For a leader, does he run single or double lead ? Does he know his commands, **GEE** and **HAW** ?
At what speed and in what size of team does he normally run ? If he has raced, what have been the results ?
How many miles did he run in the last year ?
What type of trails has he usually run on ? Has he often run in the woods ? Does he chase deer, moose, fox ?
Does he prefer to run on the right or the left ?
Has he already run in front of a sled, an ATV, a skier, a bicycle ?
Does he fear water, ice, bare ground, etc. ?
What is his present diet, his training diet ? Is he a good drinker ?
Is he registered ? Is his pedigree certified by the Canadian Kennel Club ? Can we see his health record ? Has he been injured ? Does he have a tendency towards certain illnesses ?

ALL ABOUT THE DOGS

Choosing a dog

Do not be embarrassed to contact the breeder some weeks or even months later to ask about certain particulars concerning of the dog. He ought normally to be able to help you. I must add that **I have known mushers who got dogs almost free from shelters for abandoned dogs** on the sole basis of their appearance as a northern breed. I would like to add that in most cases, the results have surpassed their hopes. I remember two ordinary looking dogs my son had bought to close a deal. They proved to be the best of the group. I did not realize until much later that the breeder had kept these dogs not because of their appearance but because of their performance.

RAISING PUPPIES

Everything depends on your ambitions. If you hope to be a champion racer, the chances of your dog producing five champions out of six pups in a litter are almost zero. However, if pleasure runs interest you, two well chosen dogs, when bred, will produce pups which will be able to pull your sled next year. I think that the socialization involved in building a team will make your task easier and you will have fewer fighters. If you have bought two experienced dogs, they will help train the young ones. One of the problems is that you will not be able to drive a sled dog efficiently before two years of age. The pups are not able to be worked hard before they are a year old, and their training will take at least another year.

This is a little long, and I suggest you buy at least four adult dogs to have good runs to begin

Ashley and Lindsay

Kennel of Barbara & David Totem, Willow, Alaska

Choosing a dog

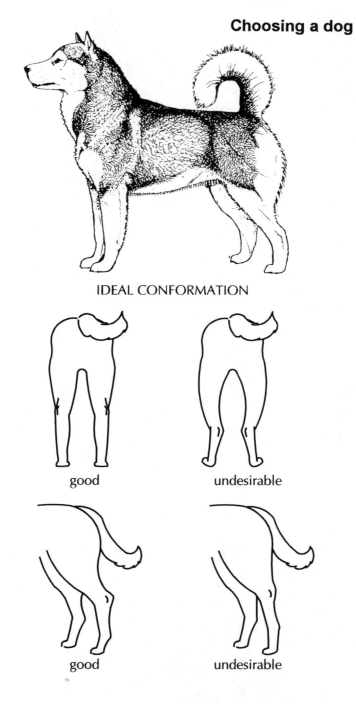

IDEAL CONFORMATION

good   undesirable

good   undesirable

Nutritional needs

Here, I will present my bias immediately. Personally, I wouldn't like to eat only dried foods, even if they were for human consumption. And secondly, I have raised dogs for thirty-five years and **have yet to see my dogs devouring a corn field !** In effect, northern dogs have been raised for generations on meat and fish. Iditarod mushers whom I had the pleasure of meeting believe, as I do, that sled dogs need to be fed with meat and fish. Having said that, I also appreciate that the majority of breeders do not have access to adequate supplies of meat and fish to feed a large group of dogs. On the other hand, I am also convinced that the addition of a good quality dry food allows the dogs to meet their dietary requirements.

The feeding of working dogs in particular has been studied as early as the turn of the century by those exploring the northern climes. Those who conquered the North and South Poles could not count on hunting or fishing alone to feed their sled dogs. Therefore, they were required to be very precise in calculating the amounts of provisions required during their expeditions. For those of you who are not familiar with the details of these expeditions, it was normal practice to leave with literally hundreds of sled dogs. Once underway and some distance into the voyage, **weaker members of the dog teams were slaughtered and used to feed the others**. By the end of the expedition it was not unusual to have only half of the original sled dogs left. The dogs remaining were those chosen as being the most efficient in changing their food into energy, requiring little water and being very tolerant of the extremely cold temperatures. This type of genetic selection provided the Nordic peoples with dogs who became the basis for the hardy northern breeds.

Nutritional needs

QUALIFYING ASPECTS

The energy requirements of a working sled dog are very high. This necessitates a food ration with a high biologic and caloric value. To be used, **foods will only be able to release their energy** once they are digested and metabolized.

* Energy must be **quickely and easily** available in order to provide nourishment at the cellular level.

* The energy balance of the various foods must be presented in a manner which will **minimize both bulk and waste** so that gastric problems do not become an issue.

* **Digestion time must be optimized.** Too short a time will precipitate problems of diarrhea. Too long a time will provoke vomiting and increase the risk of gastric torsion. The feed should be fed moistened, but not as a soup.

* The digestibility of foodstuffs must be high. Dogs can digest large quantities of protein, particularly if it is of animal origin. Likewise, **lipids (fats) constitute the preferred energy source for sled dogs**. It is also essential that carbohydrates be highly digestible.

Breeders from Québec have the good fortune to have **frozen ground chicken available** at very reasonable prices. They also can buy dry dog food in a wide range of qualities at competitive prices.

Certain breeders also have access to by-products of slaughter houses, meat processing plants, restaurants, etc.

Nutritional needs

It is very difficult to recommend a magic recipe for dog feed. **Each musher will adapt the feed for his dogs** according to availability, cost and the needs of his dogs. The activity level of the animals will also be taken into account. There are certain guidelines that should be considered :

* The dog's stomach is very **sensitive to any dietary change**. Try always to use the same type of food. If modifications are necessary, make them gradually.

* Watch each of your dogs - how they look to the eye, and what their body feels like. Weigh them often and then adjust the diet according to need (age, gestation, activities, weather, etc.). **Obesity is as bad as insufficient food intake.**

* Make sure that your **dogs drink sufficiently** and encourage them to drink by every means at your disposal.

* Check your dogs frequently for dietary deficiencies through consultation with your veterinarian or **with a veterinarian specializing in the care of working dogs**.

* Use dietary supplements (vitamins, etc) with caution so as **not to create an imbalance in the animal's metabolism**.

* Check carefully the **quality of the feed** and, definitely, don't feed foodstuffs that spoil easily. Do not give sweets, chocolate or table scraps.

Nutritional needs

The dietary requirements of your dogs will vary according to the following criteria:

* **The breed of your dogs**
* **The weight of each of your dogs**
* **The activity level of your dogs**
* **The ambient temperature**
* **The efficiency of each animal's digestive system**
* **The physical condition of the animals**

These criteria indicate the complexity of trying to suggest a standard ration. In effect, each dog in your kennel should have a diet tailored on a daily basis to his needs, taking into account the variables listed above.

To add to the degree of complexity, the availability of desired foods is also a variable. Some mushers are able to get good quality beaver carcasses, others ground frozen chicken, fish, etc. Each of these protein sources will have its own characteristics which vary according to the type of animal and the body parts used. There exists as well an enormous variety of dry dog food to satisfy the most discriminating of self made nutritionists.

I do not intend to dwell on every small detail of the management of animal nutrition. Generally, **Northern species (like huskies, etc...) consume about 80% of the food that domestic dogs do for the same level of activity**. This book is meant to be a practical guide for amateurs. I know that mushers prefer to spend more time with their dogs than in the pages of a book. This approach I agree with! However, I think that a simple method to calculate a diet would be helpful.

Nutritional needs

QUANTITY

Dogs usually have voracious appetites, easily consuming high energy foods in enormous quantities. Their ancestors passed on the survival genes which dictated that when the opportunity to eat presented itself, then the dogs would literally gorge themselves. Possibly more food would not be available for several days. **The dog's stomach has an enormous capacity to expand to accommodate the ingestion of huge amounts of food even after several days of fasting.** The gastro-intestinal tract of the husky is about six times longer than his body length. The enzyme systems in place are able to very efficiently break down both proteins and lipids. However, this biological processing machine works best with a constant and unvaried diet. Don't forget that dogs will eat almost anything put in front of them. They are not gourmets !

ENERGY REQUIREMENTS

The average maintenance energy requirements of a sled **dog of fifty-five pounds** has been estimated to be about **1500 kilocalories of metabolizable energy per day**. This has been established by the American National Research Council. These values have been found to sustain this animal during minimal activity (e.g. the animal is in a pen or is tethered), with moderate temperatures (as in fall or spring), and for the northern breeds (malamutes, huskies, alaskans).

Increasing energy requirements of sled dogs will vary with the degree of activity, the temperature, the breed, the physical condition etc. It is not surprising that nutritional experts have yet been unable to establish a uniform norm. In general, one can multiply the basic requirements by a factor of 1.5 for the moderate exercise of small races or short distance runs. For more intense exercise such as long distance expeditions this factor will be 2.5.

To meet the required energy levels, the musher must take into account two more factors.

* **The ration must be balanced sufficiently to meet each of the dietary requirements.**

* **The quantity given must correspond to the energy requirements of the dog.**

BALANCING THE RATION

Sled dogs are athletes who need to be fueled according to their activity. Even if their ancestors were mostly content with a limited variety of food (caribou, seal and fish), it is certain that many of these animals would have in fact exhibited symptoms suggesting deficiencies in their diet. These in turn probably influenced the physical condition of the animal and possibly even its life. I would suggest to you to determine the amount of metabolizable energy in the feed of your dogs. Each food has a number of components, however, energy is supplied by three easily evaluated sources:

PROTEINS
Nitrogenized acids, amino acids
LIPIDS
Fats, fatty acids
CARBOHYDRATES
Sugars, non-nitrogen extracts

Nutritional needs

NUTRITIONAL RECOMMENDATIONS				
FOR SLED DOGS WEIGHING 45 POUNDS				
	MAINTENANCE	MINIMAL EFFORT	EXTENDED EFFORT	ENDURANCE
Metabolizable Energy kcal ME/day	1000 to 1200	1500 to 2000	2500 to 5000	6500 to 8000
Proteins % ME	20 to 25	30 to 35	35 to 40	35 to 40
Lipids % ME	15 to 25	20 to 30	25 to 35	30 to 60
Carbohy-drates % ME	40 to 60	30 to 50	20 to 40	15 to 30

Fiber % DM	2 to 5	3	2.5	2
Short chain fatty acids	1 to 2.5	2.5 to 5	5 to 7	8 to 10

Kcal ME/day :Kilocalories of metabolizable energy required per day
% DM : Percentage of dry matter

It is therefore important to know the breakdown of each of the components of your feed so that you can arrive at a balanced ration. I don't want to imply that you will need a computer to manage this task. It is relatively easy to calculate the contribution of each of these elements to the final diet of your dogs.

Nutritional needs

Energy contribution as a percentage of dry matter (DM)

INGREDIENTS	DM %	PROTEIN %	LIPIDS %	CARBOHY-DRATES %
BEEF	30	70	16	--
LIVER	28	69.6	18.3	6.7
LAMB	40	37.5	60.0	--
HORSE	29	51.4	19.4	--
BEAVER	40	67.5	30.0	--
CARIBOU	37	54	28.0	--
CHICKEN	35	43.7	42.2	8.7
CARP	31	61.9	29.4	--
HERRING	26	70.4	24.5	--
PIKE	20	70.0	25.0	--
POTATOES	20	10	--	80
DRIED PEAS	89	24.9	1.5	62.7
SUNFLOWER SEEDS	93	49.8	3.1	26.7
CORN	89	10.9	4.3	80.4
RICE	91	8.0	2.0	85.5
SOYA	90	55.1	1.0	33.7
BONE MEAL	97	8.4	3.4	10.7
WHEAT GERM	88	28.1	9.5	54.2
FATS & OILS	99	--	99.0	--
DRIED MILK	94	35.8	0.9	54.6
EGGS	43	22.4	14.4	46.3

Nutritional needs

EVALUATING THE NUTRITIONAL VALUE

It is extremely difficult to exactly calculate the nutritional value of your feed mix. Exact results are really only possible with the use of laboratory facilities. However, it is relatively easy to arrive at an approximation that will allow you to make informed decisions. I suggest that you consult the HANDBOOK #8, COMPOSITION OF FOODS, AGRICULTURAL RESEARCH SERVICE, UNITED STATES DEPARTMENT OF AGRICULTURE. This text is usually available in university libraries. I also recommend that you consider buying NUTRIENT REQUIREMENTS OF DOGS (REV 1995), NATIONAL ACADEMY PRESS, WASHINGTON D.C., 2101 CONSTITUTION AVE. N.W., WASHINGTON, D.C., 20418.

Most values relative to diet are given as a percentage of dry matter. In the following calculations, I have used the net metabolizable energy values as follows:

Proteins   **1590 kcal/pound** of dry matter
Lipids   **3845 kcal/pound** of dry matter
Carbohydrates   **1590 kcal/pound** of dry matter

In effect, one only has to add together the metabolizable energy input of your feed mix, and then divide that by the number of animals that you are feeding. Note that **lipids furnish 2.42 times more calories per unit than either proteins or glucids**. The response time of lipids is also shorter, it is a highly concentrated source of energy.

Nutritional needs

METABOLIZABLE ENERGY OF DAILY RATION FOR TWENTY SLED DOGS (± 45 pounds each)

INGREDIENTS

Horse meat	25 lbs	Pike	40 lbs
Chicken	20 lbs	Rice	10 lbs
Beef liver	10 lbs	Grain	10 lbs

PROTEINS

Horse meat	25 lbs x 29.0% dm x 51.4% =	3.73 lbs
Chicken	20 lbs x 35.0% dm x 43.7% =	3.06 lbs
Liver	10 lbs x 28.0% dm x 69.9% =	1.96 lb
Rice	10 lbs x 91.0% dm x 8.0% =	0.73 lb
Northern Pike	40 lbs x 20.0% dm x 70.0% =	5.60 lbs
Meal	10 lbs x 90.0% dm x 30.0% =	2.70 lbs

$$\text{total} \qquad 17.78 \text{ lbs}$$

$$17.78 \text{ lbs} \times 1{,}590 \text{ Kcal/lb} = 28{,}270 \text{ kcal}$$

LIPIDS

Horse	25 lbs x 29.0% dm x 19,4 % =	1.41 lb
Chicken	20 lbs x 35.0% dm x 42,5% =	2.97 lbs
Liver	10 lbs x 28.0% dm x 18,3% =	0.51 lb
Rice	10 lbs x 91.0% dm x 2,0% =	0.18 lb
Northern Pike	40 lbs x 20.0% dm x 25,0% =	2.00 lbs
Meal	10 lbs x 90.0% dm x 20,0% =	1.80 lb

$$\text{total} \qquad 8.87 \text{ lbs}$$

$$8.87 \text{ lbs} \times 3{,}845 \text{ kcal/lb} = 34{,}105 \text{ kcal}$$

* Meal = commercial dry dog food

Nutritional needs

CARBOHYDRATES

Horse meat	25 lbs x 29.0% dm x	0.0%	=	0.00 lb
Chicken	20 lbs x 35.0% dm x	8.7%	=	0.61 lb
Liver	10 lbs x 28.0% dm x	6.7%	=	0.19 lb
Rice	10 lbs x 91.0% dm x	85.5%	=	7.78 lbs
Northern Pike	40 lbs x 20.0% dm x	0.0%	=	0.00 lb
Meal	10 lbs x 90.0% dm x	34.5%	=	3.11 lbs
	total			11.69 lbs

11.69 lbs x 1,590 kcal/lb = 18,587 kcal

SUMMARY

Protein	28,270	(35%)
Lipids	34,105	(42%)
Carbohydrates	18,587	(23%)
total	80,962 kcal	(100%)

80,962 kcal / 20 dogs = 4,048 kcal/dog-day

This feed mix should meet the daily energy requirements of a forty-five pound dog having a some-what demanding exercise program, i.e. expeditions of 20 to 45 miles per day. Portions fed to each animal will have to be adjusted to meet the condition and activity levels in place at that time. The values do not necessar-ily depend on the quantity used. Metabolizable energy may vary according to the part of the food source used whether one speaks of horse meat, chicken or even the type of rice. Still, using this approach will allow you to better understand how your food mix has been put together, and therefore making adjustments will be more easily accomplished without losing the essence of your diet. In dividing the cost of each pound of all ingredi-ents by the metabolizable energy that each contains, you will then be able to compare your food type costs in terms of kilocalories.

Nutritional needs

COMPARING DIFFERENT SOURCES OF METABO-LIZABLE ENERGY FOR DOGS (based on 10 pounds)

Beef (deboned) (± $0.25 per pound)

Proteins
10 x 30% dm x 70% x 15,905 kcal/lb   =   3,339 kcal
Lipids
10 x 30% dm x 16.6% x 3,845 kcal/lb   =   1,915 kcal

                total   5,254 kcal

Unit price   ± $2.50/5,254 = $0.000476/kcal

Chicken (ground) (± $0.15 per pound)

Proteins
10 x 35% dm x 43.7% x 1,590 kcal/lb   =   2,432 kcal
Lipids
10 x 35% dm x 42.5% x 3,845 kcal/lb   =   5,719 kcal
Carbohydrates
10 x 35% dm x 8.7% x 1,590 kcal/lb   =   484 kcal

                total   8,635 kcal

Unit price   ± $1.50/8,635 = $0.000173/kcal

Meal (30/20) (± $0.70 per pound)

Proteins
10 x 90% dm x 30% x 1,590 kcal/lb   =   4,293 kcal
Lipids
10 x 90% dm x 20% x 3,845 kcal/lb   =   6,921 kcal
Carbohydrates
10 x 90% dm x 34.5% x 1,590 kcal/lb   =   4,937 kcal

                total   16,151 kcal

Unit price   ± $7.00/16,151 = $0.000433/kcal

Nutritional needs

ADJUSTING THE SOURCES OF METABOLIZABLE ENERGY

Water content
Being that the metabolizable energy levels are given in kcal per pound of dry matter, a ration must have the water weight removed from the unit weight before one can proceed with the appropriate calculations. For example, if the meat has 70% water, then the weight of the meat must be multiplied by 0.30 to establish the dry matter weight.

Food management and preparation
The manner of feeding and of feeding preparation also plays a role in the metabolizable energy available in the feed mix. Excess waste is undesirable, as is food that is poorly absorbed by the animal. Many food elements lose a certain percentage of the metabolizable energy due to the manner in which they are stored or refrigerated or prepared. Cooking causes some loss of fats, but it does not change the digestibility.

Digestibility
The levels of metabolizable energy used in the preceding calculations were based on a protein digestibility of 80%, a lipid digestibility of 85%, and a glucid digestibility of 85%. This is one of the reasons that it is so important to choose the commercial grain dog foods with such care. With these foods, it is important to choose one with a guaranteed level of digestibility. Rarely does this level exceed 90%. When bears come out of hibernation, they eat vegetation. I always thought that this was an excellent way to clean the digestive system from toxins which were accumulated during the winter. I believe that dogs do this for the same reason.

Nutritional needs

QUALITY OF THE FOOD MIX

Proteins
Proteins supply the organism with indispensable amino acids - the building blocks of all protein based cells. They must be of good quality.

Biological value of different protein sources

eggs	100%
fish	92%
meat	80%
complete meals	45%

Lipids(fats)
Fats must be supplied in such a way as to be appropriately divided amongst the three types of fatty acids.

- Saturated long chain fatty acids should account for 30 - 50% of supplied fats. These fats are pure energy. They are found in the fatty tissues and muscles of mammals and poultry.
- Saturated short chain fatty acids should account for 20 - 30% of supplied fats. This pure energy source is more easily digested and converted to usable energy. They do not store well in the tissues as do other fats. Short chain fatty acids are found in oils of vegetables, coconut, copra and palm.
- Essential fatty acids should account for 10 - 30% of supplied fats. Vegetable oils of corn or sunflowers are necessary for the good health of skin and coat. Fish oils increase membrane permeability to the entry of oxygen and also have a proven anti-inflammatory effect. One of my friend suggested that certain elements in soya oil can have a depressive effect on canine thyroid function.

Nutritional needs

Carbohydrates

Starches are the main source of carbohydrates and are mainly available from plants in the form of grains, tubers, and root vegetables.

Although man requires a minimum of 15% of carbohydrates in his diet for intense activity, sled dogs can function very well with a diet devoid of carbohydrates. The glucogenic capacity of the liver and kidneys are usually sufficient to meet the metabolic need for glucose without inclusion of carbohydrate in the diet. **Incorporating more than 30% of carbohydrates as an energy source for canines during intense activity is ineffective and will result in poor performance**, as well as potentially precipitating illness and muscular stiffness. At levels of thirty percent, carbohydrates should not be used at all unless their source has been well processed and well cooked - even for dogs on a maintenance diet. Starches in effect have a very poor digestibility rate. Potatoes need to be peeled and then well cooked. The cooking process will change the starches to dextrins. Carbohydrate energy levels above 30% will cause acute diarrhea, a condition that will immediately reverse itself when the carbohydrate levels are reduced in the ration. Certain dogs seem to enjoy fruits, however, fruits do not make an important contribution to the production of energy.

Fiber

Fiber is not digested by the dog, and does not contribute to the energy cycle. Its sole purpose seems to be the creation of bulk in the gastro-intestinal tract, which in turn aids in the transit of foodstuffs through the gut thereby preventing constipation. Conversely, excess levels of fiber in the diet can be detrimental by absorbing some of the nutritive substances that are present.

Nutritional needs

ELECTROLYTES (MINERAL SALTS)

Sodium (Na), potassium (K), calcium (Ca), phosphorous (P) and manganese (Mg) are essential elements to the overall wellbeing of sled dogs. Also important are zinc (Zn) and copper (Cu). To assure that my dogs receive the minimum daily requirements of electrolytes and vitamins, I am careful to include at least one cup of commercial dog feed (meal) on a daily basis. Ideally, their diet should include (by percentage) the following mineral salts:

% DM	MAINTENANCE	MODERATE ACTIVITY	ENDURANCE
CALCIUM	1.0%	1.4%	2.0%
PHOSPHOROUS	0.8%	1.2%	1.3%
POTASSIUM	0.6%	0.7%	0.8%
NACL	2.0%	2.0%	2.0%
MAGNESIUM	0.04%	0.12%	0.15%
MANGANESE	0.03%	0.03%	0.03%

Studies done by **Dr. William Beltran** of the National Veterinarian School in Alfort, France have shown that although concentrations of these mineral salts will vary during activity, **a diet balanced in its electrolyte concentration will be sufficient for the animal without the use of supplements**. Consequently, only laboratory verification can really justify specific treatments aimed at correcting mineral salt deficiencies. It is therefore recommended not to "play" with the electrolyte puzzle and risk creating imbalances that are difficult to unravel.

Nutritional needs

Vitamins

Vitamins are not a source of energy. They do, however, play a vital role in the biochemical reactions that take place at the cellular level. These reactions in turn are those which do supply usable energy to the dog. **Dietary deficiencies or excesses can result in serious health problems to the dogs.** Vitamins B and E must be supplied to working dogs in quantities sufficient to sustain prolonged periods of working. It is believed that vitamin B12 plays a vital role in resistance to stress and also as an appetite enhancer. Unlike humans, dogs produce their own vitamin C. It has also been shown in studies that in commercial feeds, vitamin C has a tendency to oxidize rapidly resulting in a loss of efficiency within three months. The principal sources of vitamins are liver, eggs, plant seed hearts, wheat germ, yeast and vegetable oils. Many vitamins are destroyed by heat. Give them cold to your dogs. There are other vitamins and minerals which are equally essential to your dogs. Intensely working muscles will cause their loss via the urinary tract. Diets rich in fats stimulate fecal loss of calcium and magnesium.

Feed rations must also be sufficiently appetizing to the dog so that he will eat it. Even if it contains all essential elements, if the dog doesn't eat - the diet really has no value! **During periods of intense work, dogs will occasionally not eat well.** Their fatigue will influence the amount they will consume. Therefore, it is very important during these times to use rations of high energy content. I have had mushers tell me that of all types of feed, beaver meat is one that is rarely refused. Don't give your dogs table scraps. They may well appreciate these tasty morsels, but it may well result in an upset stomach, or in the worst scenario, in a vitamin - mineral imbalance.

Nutritional needs

Supplements

Some mushers will supplement the diet of their dogs when they know that their dogs will be working more intensely than usual. These supplements are mixes that supply increased quantities of the calories, vitamins and minerals that are required for increased effort. Be certain that these supplements are well balanced.

Protein supplementation 2/3
  Meat meal
  Fish meal
  Dried egg powder

Fat supplementation 1/3
  Chicken fat
  Salmon oil (purified)
  Coconut oil
  Vegetable oils

Carbohydrate supplementation
  Sugars

Refined sugars (sugar, chocolate, etc.) should not be given to dogs. The breakdown of glucose requires insulin production. One is better to use sources of unrefined sugars such as fructose as assimilation is much more rapid. (Example: dried fruits, fruit juices). Remember, however, that carbohydrates are not essential to the diet of sled dogs.

Others
  Vitamins, Minerals

To encourage my dogs to drink, I mix ground beef, liver or chicken or four tablespoons of National brand **Energy Pak®** to each gallon of water. Dogs also seem to enjoy the taste of garlic. Dogs with a lack of appetite will often eat if a bit of garlic powder is sprinkled on their food.

Nutritional needs

AVAILABILITY AND COST

The majority of experienced breeders have found the availability of good food at a reasonable cost. For the newcomer to the sport this is often not the case. It doesn't cost a lot to feed one dog. Feeding two or three is more, but still affordable even if one is buying their food at specialized shops. Then the number of the dogs in the kennel increases. The economic factor now becomes rather important. Rarely does a week go by that I am not asked to answer the simple question of **"how much does it cost per year to feed a sled dog?"** A simple question which is difficult to answer because of the complexity of variables relative to the feeding of each dog. If you feed your dogs with a high quality and high performance feed, coupled with recommended supplements, **the annual cost will be not less than $300.00 per dog**. For this reason, as your numbers grow, I suggest that you avail yourself of meat scraps available at some slaughterhouses, or purchase animal carcasses from trappers, or obtain fish from fishermen, or left-over fat from super markets or unused meats from restaurants. (Do not use oils that have been used for cooking). One caution: these products must be fresh and wholesome. If you look for these things, you will find them. And, if you do succeed, introduce these new types of food in small increments on a daily basis to allow the animal's digestive system the time to adapt. To encourage the assistance of these "suppliers", don't be shy to invite them or their children for a sled dog ride. The value of this type of public relations cannot be over-emphasized.

Subscriptions to journals specializing in dog powered sports will bring you many advantages. Many mushers, manufacturers, etc... advertise in them.

Nutritional needs

One can find ads for frozen feeds (e.g. chicken) at very reasonable rates. Companies selling commercial dog food will often have discounts listed here, particularly for those buying in larger quantities.

Raw meat

Cooking meat has the advantage of killing parasites. Raw meat is just as easily digested, and essential amino acids are not destroyed. **Do not give raw pork or bear meat.** Wild animal meat (deer, moose, caribou) should be cooked to prevent transmission of parasites. Rabbits and hares should not be given to dogs.

Bones

Opinions concerning the value of giving bones are divided. Certainly, bones are an excellent source of calcium. Bone meal is a simple way of adding the value of bones to your diet. Some mushers give only large bones to their dogs, thus preventing potential problems such as small bones lodging in the animal's throat or creating perforations in the gut. Outside of the nutritional value, **bones contribute to dental hygiene** and probably are a pleasant diversion for the dog. For hygienic reasons, do not leave old bones lying around the dog yard.

Fish

Fish is a highly digestible protein source. It should be finely minced and cooked to assure that the bones do not present any danger. Fish meal is also rich in both vitamins and mineral salts. Commercial fisheries sell frozen blocks of fish waste. Salmon, seal, carp, herring, pike, whale meat, etc... are also sometimes available in the north at an affordable price.

Nutritional needs

COMPOSITION OF THE DIET

As mushers have found by experience, scientific studies demonstrate that a diet rich in lipids (fats) if coupled with an appropriate training regime, will stimulate cardiovascular, pulmonary and enzymatic modifications necessary to promote accumulation of fat in the muscles.

This phenomenon of **fat adaptation creates an increase of 10 - 15% of metabolizable energy specifically available to working muscles.**

Because the use of fatty acids in the energy cycle produces less carbon dioxide as an end product than do proteins or carbohydrates, the respiratory system will have fewer toxins to eliminate. The rate of breathing will be more moderate. During the summer, dehydration and an increase in body temperature can literally kill your dogs. Metabolizing one pound of fats will produce 1.07 pound of water, compared to 0. 4 pound of water for protein and 0.55 pound for carbohydrates.

A simple conclusion follows. No matter the degree of activity of your dogs, **even in the summer**, give each a small portion (1 cup) of high quality (minimum 30% proteins, 20% fats + 85% guaranteed degree of digestibility) commercial meal to be certain that the minimal quantities of required vitamins and minerals are received. Keep this portion of your feed small so as not to increase the percentage of carbohydrates. Complete the diet with a high quality protein source and fats (e.g. chicken +/- 40% lipids +/-40% proteins) **so as not to lose the fat adaptation capability of the animal's metabolism.**

Nutritional needs

FEEDING

Moisten your food preparation well. This will accomplish partially rehydrating the animal, and reducing the risk of gastric torsion. Each musher will evaluate his animals' needs according to variables previously discussed. The values calculated here are a guideline only and must be adjusted according to the condition of each individual animal. **Encourage your dogs to eat immediately when they are fed**. Make sure that your food is fresh.

The timing of feeding is also important. The Inuit peoples knew that dogs did not work as well when their stomachs were full. That is probably why their dogs were always fed at the end of the day. They also on occasion, would not feed their dogs for two or three days to condition them to periods when food was not available. Even though the dog's system can adapt to this fasting condition, it is not recommended today. For dogs more than one year old, a single daily feeding at the same time each evening is ideal.

During long distance racing, dogs are better maintained if they are fed every four hours. The majority of breeders whom I have met suggest always leaving food available for puppies. This I do not do. I like to familiarize puppies with the feeding routine that they will have when they reach adulthood. I do however, feed them several small meals a day. About three hours before leaving on an outing, I like to give my dogs about a quarter of their daily food ration as well as all the water that they will take. Of course, you have to make sure that your dogs really eat their food, and in proper condition, not from the ground, all dirty.

Nutritional needs

WATER

The majority of sled dogs do not drink enough. Their daily maintenance required input of water is between 1/4 and 1/2 quart. In a short distance racing context, this input should be doubled , and in a long distance racing context, it should be tripled. **Water is, without any doubt, the most important dietary element, and also is the most frequently ignored.**

Even if water is the least expensive of dietary components, it plays a major role in metabolism within muscle cells. All mushers of experience have long understood the importance of good hydration. They will utilize all methods at their disposal to convince their athletes to drink. Think of men and women in the marathon races and how they frequently stop to drink. Dehydration in your dogs can eliminate you from a race, and your animals will need several more hours than usual to recuperate.

During the summer, I make certain that my dogs always have water available. This water must be fresh, so make certain that water is replaced daily with a fresh supply. Rinse your water bowls well and then refill them. During the winter the water will freeze in a very short period of time. Here you will benefit if you have encouraged your dogs regularly to drink well. Giving water in the feed bowl immediately following feeding is often successful, as the water will take on a bit of the flavour of the meal. This will encourage the dog to drink immediately. In addition, during the colder times of the year, **I will warm the water to about 80°F and will add small cubes of ground beef liver or frozen beaver**. This ground liver I freeze in small cube trays for easier handling later. Huskies are notorious small drinkers, so

Nutritional needs

I find it necessary to give them water in the morning as well as the evening. Otherwise I will have sled dogs that are grabbing snow while in harness! During races, it is recommended that dogs be watered several times a day to replace water loss from exercise. **Jim Welch claims that every pound lost in a race should be immediately replaced by a corresponding amount of water**, otherwise the animal is certain to have difficulty performing the next day.

How do you know if your dogs are dehydrated? Lift the skin on the back and watch how quickly it returns to its normal position. Probably you will have to try this several times before it will become a reliable tool for evaluation. If the skin returns to its normal position very slowly, you may be assured that the animal is dehydrated. If you are in a race, you would be better to replace or remove this dog from the team for the second day of competition.

Be assured that if your dogs need more feed following periods of heavy exercise, it is essential that they also have more water. This is another advantage of feeding meat. Meat has a high percentage of water (+/- 75%). **This also means that the amount of stool is reduced when you use meat as a feed base.**

The quality of water given to dogs is also important. If you are traveling, you may find that certain dogs will refuse to drink because the water will taste slightly different from that to which they are accustomed. **Never use a bowl from which other dogs have drunk, neither give a dog water remaining in another dog's bowl.** Dog bowls should be washed at least every week, mainly because it is an excellent ground for bacteria to develop.

Nutritional needs

Bacterial transmission from one dog to another can precipitate an epidemic likely to spread through your team. When you are on outings, or at races or gatherings, keep your distance from other teams. **Try not to stake out your dogs in an area where dogs other than your own have been recently.** If it is possible, bring your own water with you.

During the winter, use only tepid water for watering your dogs. This is an "energy-saving" device, in that your dogs will not be required to bring cold water up to body temperature. **As a point of interest, to obtain one quart of warm water, a dog must have ingested 20 quarts of snow and have burned about 100 kcal.** Even if you are pressed for time, no dog can perform with this type of diet! Knowing that the water given will freeze fairly quickly, if a dog doesn't drink immediately, add a bit of liver to encourage him to drink before the water freezes. Give water more frequently and in smaller quantities. This will prevent the animal from eating snow while en route, thereby slowing down the team. In the spring, I give sap from maple trees. This "water" has a purgative effect, and I believe is efficient in clearing out the accumulated toxins of the winter season. I have no scientific proof of this, but my dogs seem to appreciate it.

PUPPIES

Feeding puppies properly is of the utmost importance. When the pups are first born, make sure that each newborn has access to the bitch's milk in the first few hours of life. It is here that the puppy will absorb the antibodies necessary to protect him against disease in the first few weeks of life. Later on, if certain puppies are weaker than their litter mates, don't be shy to

Nutritional needs

intervene and ensure that this weaker member gets his fair share of the bitch's milk. One of my females fed a litter of nine puppies without any assistance, and she herself kept in good condition. If you believe that supplemental feeding is necessary for the pups, get out the baby bottles and prepare the following milk replacement :

2 egg yolks   **1 cup of evaporated milk**
2 teaspoons of corn syrup   **1 cup of water**

Serve this preparation slightly warmed in very small portions (+/- 1/4 of a cup every four hours). Don't be alarmed by the puppy's appearance, this little weakling may turn out to be a champion.

DOG FOOD BAGS
When you are buying dry commercial dog food, never forget that you are paying for two things : the food and the bag in which it is stored. Did you know that glossy paper bags often costs the food manufacturer more than 5 to 10% of the retail cost of the food. There are two easy ways to open a bag without damaging it.

1. Unglue the bottom of the bag.

The bottom of the majority of commercial bags is simply glued shut by the manufacturer. It is usually fairly simple to pull apart this glued section or even cut it apart with a sharp knife.

2. Cut the sewn closure on the top of the bag.

Most bags are closed by sewing the top of the bag together. You can simply cut the string, and pull it to open the bag.

Nutritional needs

I feel it is important to consider reusing these bags. In fact, these bags are very useful. The interior is a waxed finish which resists dampness and weakening of the paper component. Many mushers use these bags when they are picking up stools in the dog yard. As these stools will have a large water content (over 50%), you will run out of empty bags. The amount of stool will be greater for those dogs fed with dry dog foods compared to dogs which are fed with meat.

These bags are also excellent storage units for meat or fish that you wish to freeze for future use. I, personally also use these bags to store my picket lines, etc. I use them as a base under the straw in dog crates. The crates stay cleaner and are more comfortable.

Manufacturers are required by law to list the ingredients of dry food in order of importance, as well as the weight of the food, the percentage of water, etc. But be careful, its does not mean that because meat is first on the list, that meat is the main ingredient. This information allows you to better understand the quality of the product. Also marked on the bag will be the weight percentages of protein, fats, fiber, etc. Some manufacturers will also show the guaranteed degree of digestibility. For the percentage of carbohydrates, you are best to look at the company's available literature. All of this information will allow you to compare different products that your dogs should appreciate, more or less, depending on their tastes. There are exceptions, but as a rule, a 30/20 bag of dog food is a 30/20 bag of dog food (30% proteins and 20 % fats) and the price difference reflects marketing technique costs (publicity, intermediaries, presentation, transportation, profits, etc...). **I remind you that with nutrition, taste does not always represent quality.**

Cutting   *Mixing*

Feeding

Psychology

Anthropomorphism is the process of attributing to animals the moral values and feelings of humans. This is a fault which all animal lovers must avoid. Quite the opposite, the trainer must understand his dogs, know their thought processes and act in a manner which influences his dogs behavior. How can one know what goes on in the minds of these faithful friends? It isn't easy. One must learn to think like a dog. It is important to understand some basic rules which will help us to better understand their behaviour.

But be careful, this chapter does not apply to weak little beings, unhealthy and failing ones who survive thanks to medical care, to grooming clinics, special feeding programs and those whose ambitions are limited to being on a couch. This book refers rather to the noble descendants of coyotes and wolves, those animals who have savoured the taste of adventure, of action. These are dogs which form a pack, coming together for a common goal, as their ancestors have done for thousands of years in order to survive in less than favorable conditions. **They need a 'master', a leader**, just as when they lived in the wild, to maintain order, but forget about the old time "macho" use of whips. Do not use one at all, even for signaling. You will be confronted with the problems found in all societies. Each one will have his own needs, his own personality, tastes and feelings, etc.

Not easy, for ethology is a relatively young science. I recommend that you read the major works on animal behaviour (**Pavlov, Lorenz, Von Frish, Pradines**). I am convinced that this will be able to effect your own social behaviour.

Psychology

Let's clarify immediately that the behaviour of an animal reflects principally a reaction (in nature almost automatically) to a stimulus, the response following either his **natural instinct** or from **learned experiences**. A dog will follow a rabbit trail instinctively, without either his parents or a human being having to have taught him. He will chase the rabbit. He is able also to learn behaviours which are not innate. One is able to teach a dog to sit, to stop or to speed up with simply commands. There is a great difference between the reflexes of a man and of a dog. A man will have the tendency to evaluate the reason for a command, to think before acting. The outcome will be less automatic than in a dog's world.

Dogs have a sense of smell and hearing that is significant and they often react to conditions of which you have no understanding. These are opportunistic hunters, quickly distracted by new smells or unusual sounds. **Dogs react quickly without thinking of consequences**, or of the long term. Even their sight is affected by the lack of a horizon. Some leaders refuse to cross lakes or large fields which seem to them to be endless. They need limits or boundaries.

The musher's job is simply to adapt their behaviour to the requirements of sledding. When a dog tries to follow a rabbit track he is not trying to destroy the dog team. He is simply following an instinctive reaction, being natural. When he stops suddenly to urinate on a tree, it is not planned to drive you into a rage, but because his ancestors have marked their territory, in this way for thousands of years. A thorough understanding, patience, repetition and firmness will be necessary if you want to teach your dog to control his most basic instincts.

Psychology

Dogs differ from other animals only because they have developed a privileged place with man over many centuries. More importantly, some breeds have been chosen by man because they possessed advantageous characteristics for accomplishing jobs. With time and patience, you may accomplish training a Chihuahua to point out a woodchuck. However, this will be much easier with a breed of hunting dogs. One of the most important characteristics of dogs is that, unlike wolves, they are domestic animals, which by definition, depend on man for their wellbeing. It is obviously also possible to train a young wolf. But, given that his ancestors have never been conditioned by man, this will be much more difficult, and seldom makes this animal very reliable.

A dog needs a master (leader) to feel safe and secure, as there is always a leader - an alpha male - in a wolf pack. Some dogs only respect a person; others only men, or only women. Some never accept a new master. In order to work well, **a dog must know that you are going to feed him, to free him if there is a tangle in the team, give him water.** There must be no doubt in his mind **that you are the leader of the pack.** Each time that he doubts it he will try to regain control. Each of your dogs relies on you, above all, if he finds himself in unknown territory or if he is placed in a new situation. It is essential that he believe **you are always in full control of the situation.** It is extremely important that you dedicate some time daily to each of your dogs, particularly when they are young, for they will recognize you as their leader. I sincerely believe that **any dog, even the least socialized, desires above all to please his master.** However, for this to happen, he must learn behaviours which are not necessarily consistent with his innate knowledge. This is not easy. As most breeders, I think that rewards are more efficient than punishments for training. Punishment must be very light, just sufficient enough that the dog understands your displeasure. **The challenge is to understand why the dog acted in a certain undesired way and to find quickly a response which will correct this behaviour.** It is pointless to punish your dog for an hour later. **A dog doesn't reflect and remember, he reacts for the moment.** After a few minutes, he hasn't the least idea why you are punishing him. Punishment often disorients the dog, who doesn't know more than to do what ever will please its master. It is the same thing with excessive talking. It is useless to shout; your dog has better hearing than you have; it is not by raising your voice that you will correct the problem. The secret, I believe, rests in patience and, above all, in the consistency of your actions. **Don't shout 'GEE' to a dog when you are sure he will not turn to the right, and under no circumstances, you must not let him turn to the left, if you have given the 'GEE' command.** Be firm, unwavering, consistent. Do not punish a dog who has run away and that you have had a problem catching. If you do, it will be more difficult to catch him the next time. Rather, attract him with a treat when he is tethered until he comes naturally to you. You must interpret your dog's behaviour to discover a cause for its action, then to find a solution to the problem, not simply confuse your dog more. It is unusual that a dog intentionally disobeys his master, and in this case a 'NO-NO-NO' is often enough to restore order.

I like the way that the Pearces from Hudson encourage pack socialization with their dogs. Upon returning from training, all of the dogs are let loose in the fenced in kennel area. After a short free run, each dog is called by name and comes to be attached in his proper place. This is a simple behaviour to shape when the dog is rewarded with a doggie biscuit !

Psychology

Above all, try not to carry on endlessly. Not only will the guilty dog be distressed, but all the others will be also. Avoid hitting a dog. You must have all his respect. One of my friends gently twists the ear of his hunting dog and this action seems to bear fruit. If I must be severe, I am usually content to speak to the dog, shaking him a little to show him my displeasure. Obviously, the exception will be when a fight breaks out, when I intervene more energetically. I have a starting pistol to frighten intruders. **A stranger must never approach a dog extending his hand over his head.** Only the master should show his dog his authority in this way. A stranger must simply crouch (this is less intimidating) and show the back of his hand to the dog for the dog to sniff it, then he can gently stroke the dog under the chin.

COMMUNICATION

As a musher you are part of the team. Your dogs can learn some simple words and associate them with a command of yours. These connections are significantly related to your voice in particular, so that the tone in which you give the command is important. **Choose your words and never change the meaning of a key word for continuity.**

None of your dogs should have a name that sounds like one of your commands. **Names and commands must be short and clear, because dogs are not able to decipher phrases.** They respond to simple words and often only if these words are spoken by their master and in his usual tone. Given that you will surely have the occasion to buy or sell dogs, there is a great advantage in adopting the standard commands, which you will find at the end of this book.

Psychology

Remember that a dog's hearing is very keen and nothing is served by raising your voice. This cannot be stressed enough. Each of your dogs wants to please you, but he must understand what it is you want.

APPRENTICESHIP

Most dogs love to run, to investigate new areas, to join a pack and they love making their masters happy. Social behavior is the first thing they must learn. If you raise a litter of pups, keep them together as long as you can, in a large pen, to help develop their sense of being a team. They will learn at the same time to respect each other and this might limit conflicts between dogs when they are older. If you plan to keep a puppy in the house, realize that he will need to go out every four hours to eliminate. My experience with puppies makes me believe that it is almost a must to keep at least two of them. Play is of the greatest importance in the development of healthy behavior. Their socialization must involve humans. **You must make daily contact with** each puppy and take time to play with him. Ask all your visitors to pet your young dogs so that they become comfortable not only with you but also with strangers. From six weeks old, take each pup in turn with you, whether for a ride in a truck, or into the house for a few hours. At the outset, you will note that they will appear helpless when they leave the others behind in the pen. Then, gradually, they will adopt you as a friend and will want to spend time with you. Begin immediately to teach them the command "NO". As soon as they do something unacceptable, repeat quickly "NO, NO, NO" and act to prevent their continuing. Young dogs are particularly receptive and understand much more quickly what you expect from them. As soon as they are three months old, put a permanent collar on them.

Psychology

When they are comfortable with the collar, while you watch them, try a harness on them for a few minutes. At the beginning they will likely try to chew the harness. Watch closely because you do not want them to pick up this bad habit. **Never leave them unsupervised with a harness on.**

If you have an available area reasonably free of roads, add a line and weight to the harness to get them used to pulling and let them run around you so they will exhaust their craziness. Remember that a puppy is not able to work nor learn in this excited manner. Do this in short ten minute periods so the puppy will see it as an exercise, almost a game, and not a chore. Some breeders allow pups to follow an adult team. I am not sure that this is a good method. I think that this is likely to encourage their independence. I prefer to wait until they have reached four to eight months old to introduce them to a sled.

It is clearly possible, with time and patience, to initiate four pups to working in harness without the help of more experienced dogs. However, it is so much easier to have a pup understand if the owner places him in an experienced team, that this is almost essential. If you do not have good adult dogs, ask another breeder to start your pups. Personally, I arrange to have a pleasure run with 6 of my most calm dogs in order to tire them a little. Then I replace the two wheel dogs with young ones, 4 to 8 months old. I assign a person to drive the sled while I encourage the new pups. At the appropriate time I give the start command and my helper releases the sled at the same time. During the first few moments, some dogs let themselves dragged.

Psychology

Normally, it takes only a few seconds for each dog to learn that he is interested in remaining with the others. Given that the rest of the team is already tired, the pups commonly wish to run more quickly and really pull the sled. These first experiences must occur on a sliding surface, like snow, or on sand, to avoid injuries to the ones who resist. It is also extremely important that **these dogs have a positive memory of their first experience.** They must see this run as a game. It is wise for you to stop them well before they are tired. Usually, I limit their first run to a maximum of one mile.

I also systematically avoid hooking them in a team which is too large or too fast. I try to hook them up, two at a time beside each other so that they may have some confidence being with one of their own group. Distances may be lengthened gradually. Remember that these animals are still growing. Although they seem to be able to run faster, they do not yet have the physical capacity to give a sustained effort. It is important that you do not go beyond their limits, both physiological and psychological. **The run must remain a game.** You cannot force a dog to run. He must want to run and pull your sled. Even though it is the nature of this breed, dogs under one and one-half years old should not go further than 10 miles in a single run.

I have heard that one can train a team without the help of a more experienced dog. With patience, you will begin to show one of them to hold the line out while you hook up the other dogs. You will teach him also not to come back to play with you when you stop. However, it is so much easier to benefit from at least one experienced dog to drive your team that is almost essential for your own morale. If you are not able to buy one, rent

Psychology

one. It is usually easy enough to buy, at a reasonable price, an experienced dog which, perhaps is no longer fast enough for races or too old for long trips, but will be excellent for training young pups.

The ideal position for each dog in a team remains to be discovered. Some dogs love to run on the right, others on the left, and others alone. I usually hook the larger, stronger dogs in the wheel position for they absorb most of the jerks and jolts. Experience has shown that these dogs are four times more likely to have shoulder injuries than those in other positions. It is important to develop some leaders. A pairing of a male with a female usually limits fights. Develop in them an all-purpose experience, change their position regularly in case you will have to do it later. In many ways it is nearly essential to rotate the dogs positions in the team both to minimize injuries and to avoid monotony. Study the gait, the rhythm of your dogs and match them according to their speed. What is more discouraging for young huskies than to have a team of malamutes who refuse to run? Certainly, **the vast majority of dogs want to run and accept pulling a load**, but avoid badly matched teams. As a general rule, each breed has its own characteristics and it is very difficult to get satisfying results if the dogs do not have approximately the same build.

The training of lead dogs is much more difficult and requires patience, even if you have an experienced leader available. It isn't easy to teach a dog that he must turn right when you give the command. I have found a method which complements other training methods and should be associated with all the other techniques, if possible. I hook up the dogs at night. Then with my headlamp I constantly point the light on

Psychology

the dog to turn right, 'GEE', at the same time I direct the light beam to the right. I have noted that this really helps the dogs to associate the words 'GEE' and 'HAW' to changes of direction. Clearly, at the beginning, it is advantageous to arrange that the dogs will reach a 'T' where they must turn, be it right or left. Take the time to slow down and even to stop. Be sure that your command is followed, even if you must turn them yourself. Limit the size of the team to four dogs and do not make more than four such turns in a teaching session. It isn't helpful if your dogs become tired of responding to your commands. **Teach them the two commands 'HAW' and 'GEE' at the same time so that they will understand the difference.** Systematically avoid difficult situations until your dogs know the commands well.

Once your leaders have perfectly learned these commands, you will be able to move up to 'COME HAW' or 'COME GEE' which asks the dogs to make a U-turn to the left or to the right. Begin in an area or on trails which are very wide.

It is necessary to teach your dogs to meet and to pass another team. If you have two teams it is easier. In the beginning, simply stop one team and have two people hold it in place while you make sure your team passes on the right.

Normally, the driver of the overtaking team will call 'TRAIL' and the other team must stop his team and let the other pass. Some drivers wait until the leaders reach their sled, then stop their team. This helps the passing. Now behind the team, the dogs are probably tempted to chase the team ahead of them. However, it isn't normal to ask for 'TRAIL' again before several miles.

Psychology

Gradually, your dogs will become accustomed to passing a team, even while both are moving, without a problem. The same type of exercise can be used for meeting a team head-on until your dogs have learned it well.

In head-on passing, it is the custom that each team keep to the right. However, when passing from behind (unlike normal traffic rules) the team being passed must move to the left to leave room for the passing team to keep to the right.

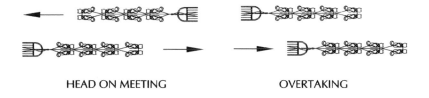

HEAD ON MEETING   OVERTAKING

Similar maneuvers must also be used for meeting or passing vehicles like snowmobiles, ATV's and above all, trucks whether the dogs be inside or outside.

Never forget to accustom your team to the public and to other teams. **Yvan Binette of Ormstown** has had a husky who trembled when a stranger approached him. To make him comfortable with the public he walked him on a leash on the main street of the local village. People came to pet him and the dog became less fearful. With patience he even succeeded in making him a leader. Use ice fishing cabans to accustom your dogs to mingle with people, stopping often, turning and retracing your path. This is an ideal place to check out their awareness. Without being too familiar with the other people, they must not show any fear. Never allow people you meet to give them food or water. This is a privilege you must guard for yourself.

Before I forget, keep with you a small bag to pick up your dogs' droppings. Your good manners will be far more appreciated than you might think!

AGGRESSIVE BEHAVIOUR

Among your dogs, as among human beings, there is range of behaviours which are more or less desirable. **Some dogs are fearful, or shy, or docile. Others are aggressive and fighters.** These behaviours are very often genetic. A fearful dog will likely have fearful puppies. Wolf offspring will have hierarchical type behaviour like its forbears. One can adapt to most of these attitudes, except for the fighters. If you tolerate these aggressive dogs, be prepared to break up fights, to pay veterinary costs, and maybe even the cost of a doctor. Imagine how many friends you will lose and your disappointment when this aggressive animal seriously injures one leader and ends his running permanently. Never bring this type of animal to competitions or to public demonstrations. In the first case, he might injure an athlete whose master has put many years into his development; in the second case, he might bite a child. My personal experience has proven to me that this type of behaviour is not correctable. I clearly don't want to automatically condemn all dogs that have been in a fight. These things happen, and there isn't much anyone can do about it. **A female in heat, an accidental injury, a strange dog - each of these can set off a fight that you will remember for a long time.** I think that if water is available it can be helpful in

Psychology

restoring order. A starting pistol is also good for stopping a war, but in some cases there is little to be done. Using a chain allows hitting dogs without injuring them, but one is not always available in urgent situations. If there are two of you, you can each grab the back feet of the two fighters, and by lifting them up at the same time, you may be successful in separating them without damage. **Never put yourself between two fighting dogs** or between two dogs who are getting ready to fight. In this case, even your best friend may bite you.

It is relatively easy to train a sled dog, but much more difficult to train a dog driver. It is certainly difficult for a musher to study the personality of each of his dogs, to understand them and to make wise decisions. However, like all the other members of the team (the dogs), the musher has his own personality, habits, preferences that he must adapt to his role of musher. Usually, the musher modifies his bad habits and can take control of his own personality easily enough. His main problem often is found at another level. **By far the most difficult decision for all breeders is to part with one of his dogs,** especially in small kennels. How is a master to come to the point of letting go a dog which often he has seen being born, and that he has trained for weeks? Nevertheless, all mushers must make this kind of decision sooner or later, and better sooner than later. Some dogs are aggressive, and every musher worth this title must not keep this type of animal, as much for the safety of other teams as for the public in general. Some claim that northern dogs are generally more aggressive than other breeds. This is not surprising, for their relationship with wolves predisposes them to the spirit of the pack, of a leader... This is not a biological weakness, it is almost normal. However, this

Psychology

attitude is not acceptable for a sled dog. I have trained for many years a team of some 20 Samoyeds. I have found them, above all, stubborn, unpredictable and very slow (this was probably because of my lack of experience). I now own a team of Siberian Huskies who seem much better team players. I have had to put away some of them who didn't respond to my expectations for different reasons, but generally I am very satisfied with them....although to assure some genetic diversity, I had to buy some pups from Alaska and New Zealand. Whatever the size of your kennel, you must one day or another make heart breaking decisions, and never hesitate to make such decisions when required. Don't believe that the situation will change. An experienced breeder told me that a fight between males may be only an accidental incident. However, when two females come to blows, they will hate each other for the rest of their lives.

Yvan Binette, Iditarod volunteer

Nadine & Polar

Psychology

Eye contact is a way of special communication between a musher and his dog. An experienced musher can evaluate both the spirit and physical condition of his dog simply by looking into his eyes.

Reproduction

Although I don't recommend to anyone to enter into a breeding program, I would have to say that there isn't a more beautiful thing than to see puppies born, to see them grow through the development of the various puppy stages, and even to see them squabble amongst themselves as they learn survival skills.

PUBERTY

Puberty is the time when major body changes and modifications in behaviour take place in all breeds of dogs, but especially in the nordic breeds, proud descendants of the wolves. A pup will squat to urinate. At puberty this same animal will remain standing and, at first, tentatively lift a rear leg at the same time. In a very short time he will lift his rear leg with confidence. At this time he will seek out specific places to urinate, a post, a tree or a clump of grass on his route; thereby leaving his scent to mark his passage and territory. Lifting a leg during urination is a complex ritual involving the delineation of territory as well as sexual capacity. Some females, especially during their heat cycle, will also lift a rear leg when urinating.

For the bitch, the appearance of blood spotting indicates the beginning of the sexually receptive time. For the first few days the female will be aggressive with the approach of males attracted by the odour of pheromones. The first heat cycle of the females is usually between the ages of six to nine months. They are able, if bred, to conceive throughout their life. The majority of breeders will wait until the second heat to breed a female. In the first stage of the heat cycle, the vulva of the bitch will swell and spotting of blood will occur. She will be very active and even flirtatious, thus drawing attention to herself. This phase lasts about ten days.

103

Reproduction

The vaginal discharge now changes from bloody to clear and yellowish. At this point, conception can take place. Now the female will accept the sexual advances of the male. The bitch will show her receptivity by 'flagging her tail' and exposing her genitals. The male will mount her and insert his penis into the vagina. The enlarged penis is locked into place by the contractile vaginal musculature. Ejaculation takes place during the time that the bitch and dog are 'tied'. The male will dismount the female during this time and turn so that he is facing away from her. **This tied breeding time can last up to 45 minutes.** During this time do not try to separate them. Following the breeding, the sperm start their voyage up the uterine horns until an ovum is found to fertilize.

The fertilized ova will attach to the uterine mucosa after about twenty days. For unplanned breedings, your veterinarian can give an injection of **Stilboesterol®** in the 36 hours following the breeding which will abort the pregnancy. This drug can precipitate in two to three weeks, the onset of another heat cycle. The period of ovulation and sexual receptivity lasts about ten days. If the female during this time is bred by different males, on different days, she will have puppies which have different fathers and different birth weights.

If the breeding is successful, a two month gestation period follows. If there is not a breeding, there is often a six week to three month period where the female will show signs of pregnancy (vaginal secretions, milk production) as hormones adjust to the non pregnant state. If you see these types of symptoms, don't worry as this is hormonal and normal. It is this phenomenon in the wild that has female wolves helping in the feeding

Reproduction

of the pups of the dominant female. Following the heat cycle, the female will enter into an inactive sexual cycle for two to 12 months (usually 6-8 months). In a pack, at the onset of the pheromones of the female in season, the males will begin battling amongst themselves for the dominant position (and therefore the right to breed). Breeding often happens with a certain amount of exhibitionism in front of the rest of the losing, silent, and perhaps jealous, males.

Males living in kennel environments with many females become accustomed to the odour of pheromones of females in season. They will usually be less bothered by the presence of such females. Needless to say, it is not wise to go to competitions or gatherings with females in season in your group. All dog drivers dream of having an exclusively male team. However, experience has shown that very often a team will have a female leader, and others in the team, as this presence exerts a calming effect on the total team. Performance of the bitch during the non-active sexual period of six months is as any male.

If she is spayed then she is good all year round! The advantages include the elimination of certain pathologies more frequently seen in breeding and unspayed bitches, such as diabetes, breast tumours and vaginal infections. If you don't wish to deal with accidental breedings and/or puppies, then sterilization of males and females is recommended. Both veterinarians and experienced mushers would agree. The animal's love of life, work ethic and endurance will not be affected. Issues of dominance and 'pecking order' will be greatly reduced.

*Naya, Avalanche, Sierra
and Monique*

Reproduction

WHELPING

Certainly you can leave the entire process in the hands of Mother Nature. Your female will probably follow the footsteps of her ancestors and have a trouble free birthing process. However, if the female in your litter is due in the winter, it would be advantageous to construct a protected whelping area.

A simple box of 3 feet wide by 4 feet long by 24 inches high raised 4 inches from the floor will be practical both for protecting as well as confining the litter. An opening of 10 inches wide by 12 inches high is an adequate size for the female to get in. If this box is then placed in a non-heated area, I suggest adding a removable roof and a 150 watt infrared lamp.

Give the female at least a month to become used to the new area. Put her food and water inside the box. **Don't add straw, newspaper or fabric pieces to the floor as this may discourage the mom from the area; and later it may even suffocate the newborn pups.**

Obviously, the female shouldn't run in harness in the last month of pregnancy. Less strenuous exercise is advisable. The whelping area should be situated in a quiet area away from kennel noises and be inaccessible to wandering dogs and cats. The female must feel secure in this new area. Still, even with all these precautions, surprises can happen. Our barn which had housed cows, sheep, goats, chickens, rabbits, etc. was transformed to accommodate a pack of Siberian Huskies. These dogs we had chosen from the better breeders in Québec and Ontario. Two of the females in this group, Smudge and Toundra, produced good quality dogs for us.

*Toundra's whelping area,
January 1996*

Reproduction

Toundra's whelping date was to be sometime between January 10th and 15th, 1994. We decided to build a whelping area in a semi-heated workshop where we had kept our sleds and wet harnesses needing to be dried.

Nothing was neglected : raised boxes of about a square meter with a removable roof, door opening slightly raised, a security board inside to protect the pups. We had thought of everything for the comfort of the new mom and the security of our future champions. A 150 watt infrared lamp with a thermostat control completed our nursery. We were finally ready.

On the 14th of January, 1994 at supper, I had to cancel a tennis game. The litter was on its way! We visited Toundra and she seemed to appreciate the support. She had already been housed in the whelping area for about a month. Friends added their predictions as to the time of birth, not this evening, it will be during the night. Weather channels announced the freeze of the century of -25°F. But we weren't worried. Huskies are made for Siberian temperatures.

Around 10:00 p.m. I was getting tired. I felt that I didn't need to worry as Toundra was quietly resting in the whelping area. I wished her good luck and retired for the night.

The following morning, about 5:00 a.m. I hurried to the workshop area with great anticipation. When I opened the door, small mewing noises greeted my ears. I ran to the whelping area, so excited! It was empty! The noises were coming from my right.

Reproduction

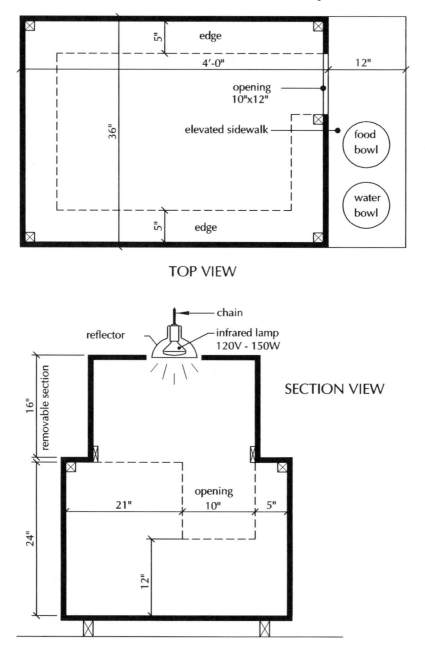

TOP VIEW

SECTION VIEW

Reproduction

Toundra was comfortably installed in my expedition sled with her new family of five little huskies battling for survival. Without a doubt, they would be **"sled dogs"**.

Normally, the mothers do not need assistance, and short of being a whelping specialist, you are better to leave her to manage the situation. Do keep an eye on her progress so you can be of assistance in case of unforseen situations. Leave cold water available and allow the bitch to go out to relieve herself from time to time.

As with other warm blooded mammals, the dog has a small window of healthy body temperature (99.3°F to 102.2°F). In the first few days of life, the puppies are kept warm by their mother. Their own temperature regulatory systems are not yet fully functional. Thermal equilibrium is maintained by the excellent heat conductibility of the blood.

Elimination of heat produced by an organism is accomplished in several ways: **by radiation, by conduction, by convection, and by evaporation of water**. The dog effectively does not have sweat glands, so heat regulation is nearly exclusively controlled through modification of respiratory rate. Dogs leave their tongue hanging out of their mouths to maximize air entry (and therefore cooling) into the respiratory system.

Although there isn't any scientific proof to back my claim, I am convinced that the first contact between puppies and their master should be in the first few days following birth. I believe that it is extremely important for socialization of the puppies that you reserve a few minutes of handling for each puppy each day starting

Reproduction

about the third day of life. This is even more important when the puppies eyes begin to open. Handle puppies gently during the first weeks of life when their psycho-social capabilities are fragile. Ambient temperature should be kept at a minimum of 50°F; more preferable would be 60°F. Keep loud noises to a minimum and don't move them to new areas. **Always leave fresh water available for the mother.** If the mom doesn't keep the whelping area adequately cleaned, wait until she is outside relieving herself, and clean the area. For the first three weeks do not put in straw or blankets etc. which could suffocate young pups or cause intestinal blockage in the mom.

With time, the mom will clean up less after her babies. It is now your turn to institute systematic cleaning of the whelping area. Begin adding some type of litter to the floor surface. I use a bed of wood shavings about 2 inches thick. This I clean two or three times a day and then replace every two days.

At four weeks of age I begin to feed the puppies with cereal well soaked in milk. Puppies should be fed several small meals per day. With the first meals, I leave the food bowl with the pups for just a few minutes. If puppies have extended abdomens which are hard even before they eat, probably your worming program wasn't effective. If they display trembling following eating, they probably ate too quickly. Excessive nutrient intake from weaning to adolescence, resulting in maximal growth rates, is incompatible with proper skeletal development.

Progressively, I increase the length of time that the mom is absent from the pups. By six weeks, she will have just one-half hour each day. Puppies are now

Reproduction

being fed commercial puppy food slightly moistened with warm water. I also give them a large bone so that they have something to chew. Chewing on bones I believe also contributes to oral hygiene.

From about six weeks of age, the pups need lots of exercise. I have found that a 10 foot x 12 foot pen with a simple dog house is ideal. I let the mom visit here at the same time as myself, to play with the pups. Toundra's last litter was nine puppies. Imagine the mayhem when you enter the puppy pen!

NAMES

What names should I give to my puppies or even a new arrival? This may seem like an easy question, but in fact it is rather difficult. Even if pups have highly developed sense of hearing, they have a strong tendency to be aware of short, crisp sounds. Train your puppies to return to you on command. It will be very usefull later on.

Ideally, a dog's name should be composed of two syllables; if only because one syllable words are limited and multi-syllable words can present complications. A dog must be able to recognize his name quickly and accurately even in catastrophic situations. Names such as **Riki, Diqui** and **Dixie** do not mix well in the same team. Always try to give names that don't sound the same. Confusion will be reduced. Examples would be **Dixie, Polar, Blackeye, Arctic, Tania, Anouk, Blizzard, Yukon, Igloo**, etc. In very large kennels, it is a good idea to adopt a theme for the names of the dogs in each litter. In this fashion it will be easy to remember the relationship between your dogs. As an example, the first litter of your bitch LASKA will bear names of

Reproduction

Alaskan cities (Fairbanks, Nome, Knik, Candle, Ruby, Kaltag, etc.) The next litter may have names of Alaskan mountains (Kenai, Chugach, Wrangell, Kinley, etc.) and the next those of Alaskan rivers (Yukon, Tanana, etc.). This way it is easy to remember that Nome is the half brother of Kenai and that their mother is LASKA. The litters of Nome may bear the names of seas around Nome (Bering, Norton, Chukchi, etc.) or of Iditarod mushers.

Do not have names which sound the same as standard commands, even if you yourself do not use these commands. The dog may be sold or exchanged with another kennel where standard commands are used. For registration of the name with the Canadian Kennel Club, the chosen name will be added to an identification name such as that of the Kennel or the blood line. **Kennel names must be approved by the Canadian Kennel Club before they are exclusively yours.**

Each of your dogs must know his name, therefore each time you approach the animal, call him by name. He will learn to associate that sound as 'his' very quickly. If you have more than twenty dogs, this exercise is also a way of greeting everyone when you visit the kennel. If you wish to change the name of a dog, this is also possible. Just repeat the new name to the animal several times a day for two or three weeks, he will learn to recognize it. Don't forget that voice tone as well as the way a name is pronounced are important to the dog. Not only does he recognize that you are addressing him but he will also know what your mood is. **Don't raise your voice, this will be interpreted as a loss of control on your part.** Some dogs will respond to their name only when it is spoken by their master.

Health & Care

This subject could fill a book by itself, but if you respect certain elementary rules, these dogs will not be too finicky. The first rule will always be to keep your kennel clean. Hygienic conditions of the kennel must be impeccable. Clean up stools on a daily basis. Disinfect the area on a regular basis. As much as possible keep the same dog in the same dog house and in the same box in the truck for transport. Clean them on a regular basis. This approach reduces transmission of bacteria between dogs. Keep a good working relationship with a veterinarian specializing in the health management of sled dogs. Veterinary medicine is a complex subject. It treats different species of animals, each with different characteristics and needs. For this reason a certain degree of specialization can be advantageous. **Each of your dogs should have a health record where medical or health issues can be noted.**

Breeds of dogs used in sledding are usually very resilient in the face of work, cold weather and general diseases. However, given that these animals not only work hard, but also frequently, there is obviously a greater chance to see some injuries. I do not wish to replace the veterinarian. I do, however, believe that all dog breeders must have a certain knowledge and ability to cope with situations requiring rapid intervention. A first aid kit is an integral part of sled dog equipment. Keep away from nutritional supplements which often can do more harm than good. And, regardless of your knowledge level in animal health, **maintain a permanent working relationship with a veterinarian specializing in health care for working dogs.** This is essential to the global well being of your team. **"You need to find a veterinarian who will show you how to fish instead of just selling you fish".** As in all professions, there are those whose goal is just to make money and others who will go out of their way to assist you. Finding a veterinarian who offers his services at a reasonable rate (not easy); finding one with experience in sled dogs (a little bit harder); finding one who will have pity for you and your sled dogs (being equivalent to winning the lottery three times in a row). When you find this ideal vet, hitch him to your kennel.

Injuries

The majority of dog drivers know the behaviour of each of their dogs so intimately that any minor variation will be immediately evident. **Experienced mushers are able to detect problems even by visual examination of stools.** Perhaps a formal diagnosis will not be forthcoming, but persistent changes in how a dog walks or runs can be indicative of a problem. In this situation, the first thing to do is to load the dog in the sled for his own ride until you are in a place where his injury can be adequately assessed. The severity of the injury will dictate whether the dog needs veterinary care or simply needs rest to heal. The type and seriousness of injuries is so variable and complex that it is not possible to look at it in any depth in this type of book. I think that breeders must use good judgement and make decisions in a reasonable period of time.

The most frequent injuries are simple cuts. It may be a deep cut, a superficial one or a long one, etc. First level intervention is to clean the area thoroughly with hydrogen peroxide and to stop any bleeding by using pressure. If it is a long cut, suturing is probably indicated. This is not difficult. Shave the fur away from the area of the cut, lift the skin and examine the cut. If it is superficial, you are best to leave it open to the air. This and the dog licking the area will speed healing.

Health & Care

Contusions are another type of injury. Bruising, without breakage of skin, occurs with some types of impacts. Evaluation of these injuries is more difficult because of its internal nature. Disinfect the wound with an antiseptic solution and let the dog rest. Fractures are relatively frequent. As in other injuries, if you are dealing with open fractures, clean and disinfect the open area, then splint the leg until you are able to seek veterinary assistance. Obviously and sadly, spinal fractures will result in the loss of your faithful companion.

Harnesses transfer the weight and pull of the sled directly to the shoulders of the dog. Reducing the incidence of shoulder injuries means reducing the incidence of sudden stops or jerks. Use a shock line at the front of your sled. Make sure that your braking system is a type that won't hook onto obstacles in the trail and cause a sudden stop. Training programs are indispensable; dogs in good condition are less prone to injury. **Dr. J.P. Belanger** suggests that a massage is probably the best treatment for injured shoulders. It is always better to prevent injuries than to have to deal with them, so help your dogs and try to keep them out of situations that will create injuries.

As for humans, food supplements, chemical substitutes, antibiotic ointments, etc... should be used with great caution. Do your dogs need it to heal a bad wound or temporary disease, or are your expectations too high ? Are your dogs companions, or slaves to be exploited ? I wonder if dogs really want to win race after race. I am not sure that it is very healthy for dogs to run 100 miles a day. Human athletes chose to disturb their health to win a competition but natural animal behaviour never goes to such extremes.

Health & Care

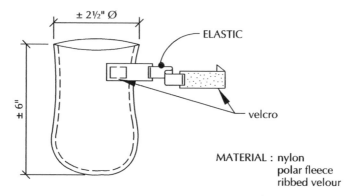

ELASTIC

± 2½" Ø

± 6"

velcro

MATERIAL : nylon
polar fleece
ribbed velour

Feet

Dogs' feet are without a doubt the anatomical part most at risk for injury. Genetics play an important role, but the musher's judgement is also essential. **Most foot injuries happen while the team is going down hills.** It is better to brake a bit on downhill sections of the trail to ensure the well-being of your dogs, and especially of their feet.

Boots must be worn if dogs are working on gravel surfaces, pavement or if the temperature is colder than -15°F. If dogs present problems with snomballs on the feet, than they should be booted. Run your hand over the surface of the trail. If it is rough to the feel, it would also be advantageous to boot up your dogs. Boots should be avoided on very soft trails. On icy surfaces boots will reduce traction and therefore will increase the risk of other injuries. In general, wearing boots will reduce the speed of the team by 1 mile/hr. Size your boots to each animal's feet. Too small will limit foot extension. Too large and the dog must run as though on snowshoes. When putting the boots on, tighten the velcro closure enough so the boot won't fall off, but not so tight to interfere with the blood circulation of the foot. Remove the boots about every four hours to ensure that

Health & Care

holes are not present where snow could enter and ball up on the foot. Some mushers use **Hooflex®** ointment to prevent the forming of snowballs on the feet.

During training before snow, pay attention to your dogs' feet if running on paved surfaces. **Pavement is extremely abrasive to dogs' feet** and can ruin the foot pads in a very few miles. Crushed stone surfaces are equally destructive. The small pieces of stone are not unlike slate and will cut the foot pads very easily. Trails with a cover of leaves or needles from conifers give ideal surfaces. Sand and gravel is also acceptable. Still one must assure that mud or sand doesn't remain between the foot pads at the end of the run. If you are running dogs on salted (calcium) or sanded surfaces, don't forget to rinse this off the feet when the training is finished.

Foot injuries are the easiest to detect and also to treat. Cuts must be cleaned with an agent such as hydrogen peroxide and then thoroughly dried. Apply an analgesic balm or an antibiotic ointment. Approximate the edges of the wound, then glue a piece of **Moleskin®** over the wound with either tissue glue or **Crazy-glue®**. Keep the patch small, and do not exceed the size of the foot pad. Finally put a boot on to protect the foot and wound as well as to prevent the dog from pulling off the patch.

The second type of injury which is nearly as frequent, is much more difficult to see. Following each outing you should always check for inter-digital abrasions. These, as well as cuts, should be cleaned with hydrogen peroxide, dried and then have an application of antibiotic ointment. Use boots on animals with these types of injuries until the feet are completely healed.

ALL ABOUT THE DOGS

Health & Care

Adding ½ ounce of gelatin to the daily feed ration of each dog will reduce inter-digital lesions. There exists an enormous variety of ointments available for foot care. For example, a mixture of zinc oxide and an antibiotic ointment is often used by distance mushers. The cost of these ointments can be high. **Dr. Del Cartec, DVM** recommends the following mixture: 3 pounds of **Vaseline®**, 1 pound of lanolin, 1/2 pound of glycerine (to prevent freezing), 70 CC of **Betadine®**, 4 tablespoons of DMSO 90% and 4 tablespoons of Dexamethasone (available by prescription). With appropriate training, good nutrition and regular surveillance, you should be able to keep your dog's feet in good condition. If you do not have foot problems, then using the above mentioned treatments should be avoided to prevent becoming dependent on these products.

Dogs who have a lot of fur on the bottom of their feet are apt to have problems in the winter with snowballs and in the summer with mud balls. In effect, the dogs don't need this fur under their feet. Use an electric razor to cut it off. It is easy and will prevent undesired problems.

Health & Care

FOOT INJURIES IN SLED DOGS

Inter-digital Cuts

Apply an antibiotic ointment
without cortisone such as
Amoxycillin®,
after having disinfected
the cut.

Worn Down Foot Pads

Apply an antibiotic such as
Amoxycillin® to worn
areas and then glue a piece
of **Moleskin®** in place.

Torn or Split Nails

Cut the ragged ends of the
nail so that it does not touch
the soil. Disinfect the
area and apply
a bandage.

Sensitive Feet

Some dogs have
sensitive foot pads
that are susceptible to
inflammation.
Apply an antibiotic
ointment mixed with
zinc oxide (**Zincofax®**).

Health & Care

Depending on the activity level of your dogs as well as the surface on which the dogs are kenneled, it may be necessary to cut the nails. When the foot is flush to the ground, the nail should not touch the surface. **For cutting, use a guillotine type nail cutter.** Cut only a small cut at a time until you are close to the end of the artery that runs down the center of the nail. Stop before you cut this living part of the nail! If this is cut, you will need to use a hemostatic powder or a silver nitrate stick to stop the bleeding.   Split nails can be repaired with **Crazy-glue®**.

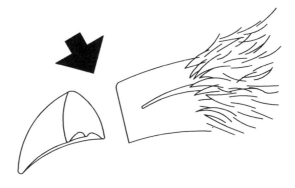

ILLNESSES

Is the dog sick ? Sometimes this is difficult to evaluate. If he could talk, the dog might tell you that he has a headache, or has a stomach ache. However, he cannot, so you will have to figure out the problem.

Aspirin® is often used for pain relief, or even to reduce stress. It can also cause gastric ulcers and may even cause the death of your dog. Use aspirin with restraint, and remember that it is not permitted in a

Health & Care

racing context. The analgesic and anti-inflammatory effects can often mask injuries that may have been underestimated by the musher. Veterinarians usually will suggest one tablet every six hours for a 55 pound dog, always given with food.

If you note a behavioural change in your dog, the first thing to do is to measure the rectal temperature with a medical thermometer. For an adult husky, the temperature will range from **100.7°F to 101.7°F**. If it is outside these limits, the dog has a problem. If this is coupled with other symptoms such as vomiting, diarrhea, or lack of appetite, a visit to your veterinarian will be necessary.

It is easy to monitor a dog's pulse rate. Just press your fingers over the artery on the inside of the rear leg. A pup will have a pulse of 110-120 per minute, an older dog 70-80, and a young adult 70-120 depending on his activity level.

A young resting husky will have a respiratory rate of 18- 20 breaths per minute. For an adult this will be 16-18 and for an older dog 14-16.

Other factors must be equally well monitored. Does your dog scratch himself a lot? Does he eat well ? Are his muzzle and nose warmer or dryer than usual ? If you clean your kennel daily, you will practically be able to diagnose problems simply from the appearance of the stools.

Given the number of dogs in a mushing kennel, managing health care should be able to be standardized.

Health & Care

INTERNAL PARASITES (WORMS)

Even if you take the best care and precautions, your dogs will probably still be infected with certain digestive system parasites. These could include :

Round Worms

These resemble long pieces of spaghetti and can be found in either stools or vomit.
Young pups with an distended abdomen most probably have round worms.

Tape Worms

There are many varieties of tape worms. Their presence will be detected either as small pieces in the stool or attached to the fur in the anal region. These small pieces or segments resemble grains of rice.

Whip Worms

These parasites cause diarrhea and weight loss. They measure about 2 inches long and have the appearance of a whip.

Hook worms

Undetectable to the naked eye, hook worms measure ± 1/2 inch long. They cause anemia through blood loss. Other symptoms can be hemorrhagic diarrhea or black stools.

Health & Care

VERMIFUGE PROTOCOL

1 - **Prevention**
* Maintain good hygiene.
* Treat for fleas, lice, etc.
* Don't feed raw meat, or offal from pigs, sheep, rabbits or chickens even if cooked.

2 - **Control**
* Analyse the stool every six months.
* Do routine deworming.
* Put new dogs into quarantine until they can be checked.

3 - **Reproductive**
* Deworm the mother 15 days prior to whelping and every two weeks from the second to eighth week after whelping.
* Deworm puppies starting at the tenth day, each week for six weeks and then once a month until the age of six months.

4 - **What to give**
* You have to use medication that is effective for most types of internal parasites. I recommand
Fenbendazole® (granules)
Ivermectin® (liquid)
Benzelmin® (liquid)
Mebendazole® (pills)

VACCINATION

Certainly there are northern dogs which have died of old age without ever having been vaccinated. However, one must also add that many other dogs have succumbed to diverse illnesses. Dogs living in the far north by their very isolation are far less exposed to the many and varied viruses that we have in the south. It is essential for most of us that our dogs be vaccinated. All municipalities and major events require that dogs present be vaccinated, particularly against rabies.

Sled dogs are particularly susceptible to pick up diverse illnesses for the following reasons :

> *** They are frequently in contact with other dogs from other areas especially on the racing circuit.**

> *** They are often working long distances on trails that are also used by wildlife.**

> *** Occasionally they may ingest contaminated food or water.**

Most rabies vaccines are good for three years. In Québec, annual vaccination against rabies is recommended. (The vaccine should be given in the summer when dogs are more at rest). Other viral infections such as distemper, hepatitis, leptospirosis, parainfluenza, adenovirus, parvovirus, etc. are dealt with through combination vaccines. It is recommended that they be given annually. My veterinarian, **Dr. Marc Quenneville, M.V.** (Veterinary clinic, St-Anicet 450-264-3790) comes to my kennel each year at the end of June for the general physical examination and vaccination of all my dogs.

Health & Care

Puppies are more complex in their health care. They are particularly vulnerable to viruses at about ten weeks of age. It is at this time that the immune effect of antibodies that the pups received at birth from the first milk (colostrum) begin to lose their effect. A clean pen protected from the rain by a roof, clean and fresh water and proper nutrition are essential elements for the prevention of illnesses. **Dr. Robert Stear** from Norden Laboratories recommends vaccinating against distemper at about six weeks of age and then also against parvo virus at the ages of nine and twelve weeks. At sixteen weeks, give a combination vaccine. Rabies vaccine should be given at about three or four months.

Parvovirus, without a doubt, is the nemesis of all mushers. Antibodies present in the mother's first milk will provide some protection to the pups (if the mother has been vaccinated). The strength of the vaccine used also plays a role. As the level of maternal antibodies present in the pups diminishes, the pups will be more and more at risk. Determining the exact point in time when maternal antibody levels are ineffective is not possible, so one must use an average age as a guideline. Your veterinarian will also be able to give advice concerning the prevention of kennel cough, heart worm prevention or other types of problems particular to your region.

Some precautions are recommended. Isolate your puppies completely from the rest of your kennel. Discourage visits from persons who have come from or visited other kennels in the previous weeks. If possible, reserve a set of clothing, boots and utensils for exclusive use around the pups.

MAINTENANCE

Dogs usually keep their fur clean. Obviously this is easier for them in a clean environment. Twice a year huskies will shed their fur and develop a new coat. During this two to three week shedding period, the dogs should have the old fur brushed out daily. This speeds up the process of ridding the dog of his old coat.

If you have just one or two dogs, giving them a regular bath becomes an option. You too will appreciate this, especially if they are in the house with you or in your car. Once you have a dozen or more dogs, this option is not as simple. With this many dogs, it is not often that the whole pack is permitted in the house or in the car at the same time, so baths too can be spaced. If your dogs are kenneled outside, obviously you won't bath them in the winter unless you have a heated area where they can be kept for a minimum of 24 hours while their heavy winter coat dries.

Most mushers never bath their dogs. Personally, **I bathe each dog twice a year, once in the spring and once in the autumn**. Baths in the summer are not recommended as the odour of soap will stay in the fur and attract insects. I use tepid water (95°F) and a mild liquid soap. Following the bath, the dogs should be kept in a clean area where they can't immediately roll in the dirt and get dirty again. Two people working together make it easier to dry the dog thoroughly after the last rinse. Dogs usually adapt quickly to bath time. Take advantage of this one-on-one operation to make a brief physical exam, look for the presence of parasites or old wounds, and to weigh the dog. Record this information in his dossier.

Health & Care

INSECTS

Nordic breeds are equipped with a thick coat to keep them warm in cold temperatures. This same coat also protects them against heat and flies. There are however, two vulnerable areas: the muzzle and the tips of the ears. Notable is the fact that the flies usually are more attracted to weaker animals. Mosquitoes are an intermediate vector for heartworms. I have tried different insecticides, sometimes mixed in an oil base; never with great success. I now use **Skin so soft**® from **Avon**® on the affected spots. This seems to help.

My dogs are kenneled in a wooded area. If they were on an open hill with a constant wind, there would be fewer insects, but more direct sun. The cleanliness of the kennel coupled with spraying the surrounding trees with an insecticide will help tremendously to contain the problem. If you keep your dogs clean with at least one bath in the spring, brush them regularly, and keep your kennel clean, insects should not constitute a major problem. Still, **if you have a dog constantly scratching, probably some type of insect is the cause**.

Fleas on dogs are not a danger to people, and are easy to eliminate with an insecticide powder. For lice, the problem is more difficult due to the rapid reproduction rate of these insects. With these, one must turn to a liquid insecticide, more precisely, **Vetkam**®, and treatment must be repeated until the lice are eradicated. Most insecticides should not be used on puppies under 8 weeks of age.

Although more rare, ticks are parasites found at the base of the ears, in the neck region, between the toes, and in the armpit area. If you attempt to pull these insects off, the head of the tick will break off and be left encrusted in the skin where it can cause an infection. You are better to apply a drop of alcohol to the tick, then in his sleepy state, when you pull on its body, the entire insect should come out.

With parasites, it is important to recognize the problem early and treat it immediately and repeatedly until the infestation is eliminated.

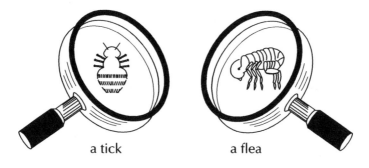

a tick   a flea

SITE ROTATION

For springtime, I usually move my dogs to a new area. I try to find a dry area, then put down a thick layer of wood shavings. In mid-summer I repeat this operation. In this fashion the soil has a chance to recover from the constant presence of urine and fecal matter. Relocating dogs with their dog house does not require a large output of time. One advantage is that the dogs seem to appreciate a new area to explore, so they have a physical as well as a psychological benefit.

Health & Care

Both hyperthermia and hypothermia can cause the death of your dog. Knowledge of the symptoms of each is essential so that you can intervene appropriately if necessary. The instrument of choice is a good rectal thermometer. Normal temperature ranges from 100.7°F to 101.7°F.

HYPERTHERMIA
Symptoms :
* The animal's mouth is wide open as he is gasping for more air.
* He shows respiratory distress.
* He will have a staggering and unsteady gait.
* He may vomit ingested water or food.
* Temperature will be above 104°F after thirty minutes of rest.
* He will have diarrhea.

Interventions :
* Cool down the animal by putting snow or cold water on the neck and belly areas until the rectal temperature drops below 103°F, before transporting.
* Give him at least two days of rest before the next out-trip. Then only exercise him if the ambient temperature is less than 50°F.
* Remember that dogs will not recall this experience. At the next outing even if the temperature is mild, the dog will still work and pull as though it were -40°F.
* Don't run your dogs if the temperature is higher than 50°F. In autumn choose early morning or late evening to run when the temperature is more reasonable.

HYPOTHERMIA

Symptoms :
* The animal is curled up and does not respond when patted.
* He will refuse to get up or even to move.
* He will exhibit shivering.
* Rectal temperature will be less than 98.6°F.
* An injured dog may also shiver.

Interventions :
* Wrap the animal in a warm blanket and put him in a warm environment. If an inside warm environment is not possible, put the affected dog in a small area with two other dogs.
* Give him warm bouillon in small and frequent quantities.
* Increase the fat content in his food.
* Check that he has adequate circulation in his lower legs and feet. Massage his body to stimulate the circulation.
* Warm highly exposed areas such as the bellies of females or genitals of males.
* Use a coat for future outings if it is particularly cold.
* If it is very cold, do your runs at night and allow the dogs to rest in the sun during the day.

Rosée

Health & Care

FIRST AID KIT

Emergency care booklet
Aspirin®, 90% alcohol, strong iodine solution, hydrogen peroxide
Polysporin®, antibiotic ointment
Anticholinergic & anti-itch cream
Algyval® Massage balm
Bandage compresses of different sizes
Absorbant cotton & dressings
Neo-atropec® for diarrhea
Adhesive tape and tensor bandages
Tweezers, safety pins, needles, sutures
Anti-inflammatories
Crazy-glue®, **Moleskin®** (**Dr. Sholls®**)
Amoxycillin® Antibiotic Cream for feet

Personal Medications

Cépacol®, **Laryngets®**, lozenges for sore throats
Oragel®, ointment for toothaches
Antibiotics and anti-inflammatory medications
Diapect® in case of diarrhea
Eye and ear drops
Polysporin®
Laxative medication

Tools

Rectal thermometer
Disposable syringes
Nail cutters
A pair of scissors
An electric razor

Musher's workshop

EQUIPMENT

The Kennel

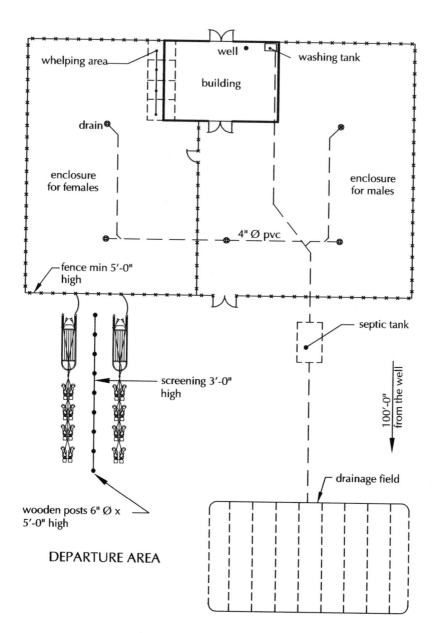

whelping area

well

washing tank

building

drain

enclosure
for females

enclosure
for males

4" Ø pvc

fence min 5'-0"
high

septic tank

screening 3'-0"
high

100'-0"
from the well

drainage field

wooden posts 6" Ø x
5'-0" high

DEPARTURE AREA

The Kennel

Does the ideal kennel exist? In fact there is not just one ideal kennel, but one for each musher. Your ideal kennel will depend upon a variety of factors, and, even then some of them will change over the course of years. Characteristics must be adapted to each geographical situation, to the number of dogs you own, to the type of activities you plan to do and, above all, to the amount of money you have available for this activity.

I have visited hundreds of kennels, each having tried to make the best that their resources would allow. One thing is clear, **the most important quality, regardless which kennel, is its cleanliness.** You have the choice. Clean it up each day as though important visitors were arriving before evening. You will then not be embarrassed to meet these same people the next day. Or, think of the cleaning as a chore, be ashamed when visitors arrive, and also be prepared to spend more money on medication to combat the results of poor hygiene in your dogs.

Don't forget, above all, that you will have to spend more than an hour each day in the kennel; that you will have to interest your family and your friends in your new hobby. Try to begin in the right way, with a good plan and a realistic vision. Try to put in place immediately the elements of your ideal kennel.

We are living in a society which is becoming more and more regimented. Well before drawing up the plans for your kennel it is wise to obtain answers to some questions, and then to decide if the place you have chosen is satisfactory for your requirements.

The Kennel

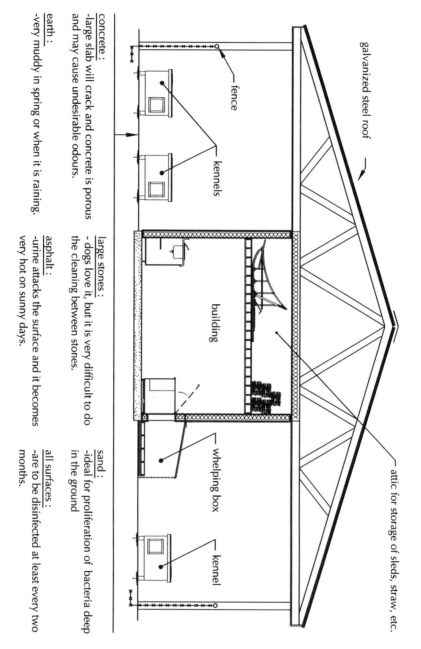

galvanized steel roof

fence

kennels

building

whelping box

kennel

attic for storage of sleds, straw, etc.

concrete :
-large slab will crack and concrete is porous and may cause undesirable odours.

earth :
-very muddy in spring or when it is raining.

large stones :
- dogs love it, but it is very difficult to do the cleaning between stones.

asphalt :
-urine attacks the surface and it becomes very hot on sunny days.

sand :
-ideal for proliferation of bacteria deep in the ground

all surfaces :
-are to be disinfected at least every two months.

138

The Kennel

LOCATION

Do municipal regulations allow the installation of a kennel ?
Is this site already contaminated by chemical products or situated in a non healthy environment (industries, waste treatment plant, etc...) ?
Do I have the right to construct a building ?
What will it cost to construct an efficient kennel ?
Will theft become a problem because of the isolation of the kennel ?
Does the site chosen drain well and is it protected from flooding, high winds, etc. ?
Will present houses, and any future houses, be a reasonable distance (1/2 mile) from your kennel so that the barking and other sounds from your dogs won't become a public nuisance ?
Are essential services available, such as water, sewage system, electricity ?
Is the proposed site accessible year round, and close enough to your home so that you will be able to get there each day ?
Is it possible to lay out trails for training your dogs, as easily in winter as during the other seasons ?
Can the site be enlarged to accommodate more dogs, or to park a trailer ?
Will the planned kennel have any resale value ?

EQUIPMENT

BUILDINGS AND NEEDS

Washable floor, walls and ceiling for maintaining proper hygiene.
A supply of fresh water for drinking as well as for cleaning.
A freezer for keeping dog food.
A storage space for bags of dry dog food.
Indoor/outdoor pens and houses for newborn pups and their mothers.
Cabinets or cupboards for storage of harnesses and other gear.
An area for the storage of straw and wood shavings.
A site for composting dog excrement or a storage area before taking it elsewhere.
Cabinets for medications, small workshop for making repairs.
An area to store sleds, gigs or all terrain vehicles (ATV).
A sink, drains, electricity, an alarm system against trespassing.
A tool bench with medium size vice and necessary tools to do small repairs.
An area for isolating new dogs for a period of time (quarantine) to assure their good health.

The Kennel

ENCLOSURES - PENS

A pen made of chain link fencing for avoiding accidental breedings by keeping bitches in season protected from visiting dogs or a dog from the kennel who breaks his chain.
A fenced area to ensure the security of dogs who may have gotten loose.
A large well anchored post, used for hooking up a team and making the departure as easily as possible.
An enclosure to allow the dogs of a team to be loose together, to get to know each other.
The base of the fence must extend down below ground level to avoid a skunk, for example, being able to get into the kennel and do its thing, or a ground hog or porcupine getting in to "needle" your best friends.

DOG YARD REQUIREMENTS

An area no less than 5 feet in diameter is required for each dog.
Houses raised above ground with a flat roof allow easy cleaning.
A permanent bowl, safe in freezing temperature and washable.
A snap, for connecting the dog to its chain, must be both efficient and secure.
Dry ground covered with wood shavings.

The Kennel

DOG YARDS

Many small breeders do not have sufficient space or means to carry out the installation and future expansion of a dog yard. I moved two houses into a corner of my barn, which are very useful for the first month of a litter of puppies, even during winter. Moving two houses inside allows relative comfort, even during winter, without too great a loss of heat. The dimensions of these houses have been chosen as acceptable for huskies (female ± 42 lbs.) A small wooden platform must be planned for the outside pen to prevent the dogs having to lie on a concrete floor.

The interior floor is elevated and insulated to make the puppies comfortable. I have used this type of set up for many years and am very pleased with it. The only real problem is the lack of space for the pups to stretch their legs. Also, they must be moved to a different set up once they reach six weeks old. **Do not make the dog houses any larger, because the dogs will fulfill their needs inside the house.** The center partition is removable, so I can sometimes give more space for one litter when they get older. During the winter I also give them fresh straw each week. If the exterior pen is not paved, use wood shavings on the ground to make cleaning up easier.

A partition is put in the dog house, with an elevated opening to prevent the puppies from getting out too soon. When it becomes very cold, I use a 100 watt electric light in this dog house to add a bit of warmth. This light bulb must be protected with a steel shield so that the dogs don't burn themselves on it.

The Kennel

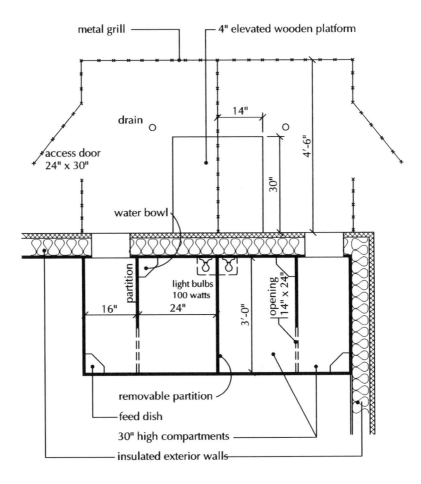

TOP VIEW

FACILITIES FOR 2 LITTERS OF PUPS

143

The Kennel

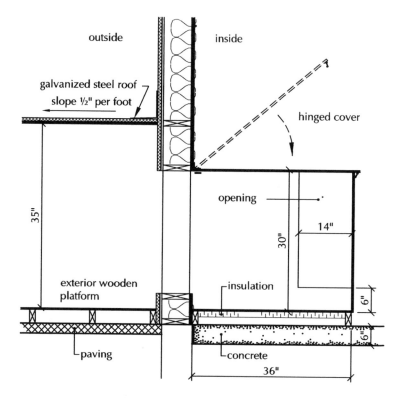

outside   inside

galvanized steel roof
slope ½" per foot

hinged cover

opening

35"

30"   14"

exterior wooden
platform

insulation

6"

paving

concrete

6"

36"

SIDE VIEW

FACILITIES FOR 2 LITTERS OF PUPS

The Kennel

SITES

There are 999 ways to kennel and attach a sled dog and if you love problems, let your imagination loose. Certainly, you can use all kinds of connectors to make your job easier and, consequently, to encourage laziness. And then, the more complicated your style of attaching your dog, the more you must invest in time and material, and the more you leave yourself open to breakage. I have met many experienced mushers who have **advised me to put my energies into training my dogs, instead of wanting to re-invent the wheel**.

Use a simple steel post, 1-½ inch in diameter, rising 6 feet from the ground. Putting a cap on the post will prevent the ring from flying off and water from accumulating into the hollow center of the post. To this attach a chain with a 3 inche diameter ring which slides on this post. This combination will hold any well conditioned and active dog. Even given that the tension of the dog exerts most of the time keeps the ring a bit above the ground, therefore the post will stay straight, even if it is not deep in the ground. On rocky ground, it is always possible to build a small concrete base of 24 inches x 24 inches x 6 inches which ought to be adequate to hold the wildest of dogs.

Even if your dog jumps to the roof of his house, the ring will stay just above the ground, even when the snow reaches 3-4 feet deep. The length of the chain, of course, depends on the space available. A minimum length of five feet seems to be agreed upon by experienced breeders. Do not skimp on the quality of the ring, the connecting snaps, or the chain. Nothing is more disagreeable, or more dangerous, than to see dogs which are loose because of poor set up of equipment. Trees in the area may succumb with time to the build up of urine in the soil. An exception seems to be cedar trees.

The Kennel

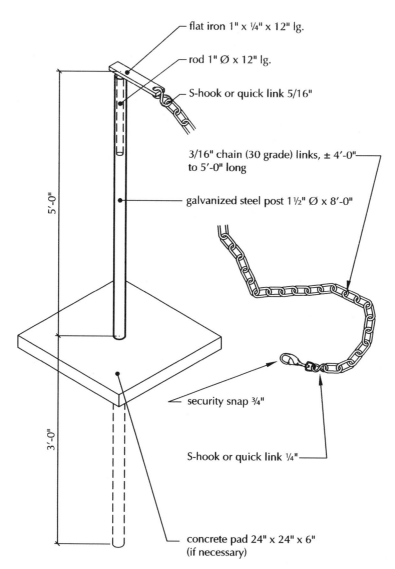

flat iron 1" x ¼" x 12" lg.

rod 1" Ø x 12" lg.

S-hook or quick link 5/16"

3/16" chain (30 grade) links, ± 4'-0" to 5'-0" long

galvanized steel post 1½" Ø x 8'-0"

5'-0"

security snap ¾"

3'-0"

S-hook or quick link ¼"

concrete pad 24" x 24" x 6" (if necessary)

SIMPLE ATTACHMENT
FOR A PUP 3 TO 9 MONTHS

Willow

The Kennel

The dog house must be at least 20 inches from the post to allow the dog to be able to pass between the two and also to be able to jump to the roof of his house without problems. Your dog should not be able to go totally around his area at the end of his chain.

In Alaska, most dogs are attached to a wooden post about 6 inches in diameter which rises about 5 feet above the ground. A chain slides around the post, giving the dog a personal space of about 5 feet in diameter. Breeders use, as we do, Italian bronze snaps. One of them claimed that, as with his experience, there is about one breakage per week (for a kennel of 100 dogs).

I prefer a security bull snap which is much stronger. Although its reverse mechanism makes it harder to open and close, it is much more secure. In fact, since I have used them, not one of my dogs has been able to open the snap and get loose. Other systems are as efficient, but a little more complicated.

During winter, following temperature variations, the surface around the dog posts might become very icy. You must not, above all, use melting chemicals (calcium) or sand (abrasives) which may damage the pads of your dogs' feet. Watch the temperature closely and just before the surface refreezes, spread out wood shavings. Straw must be used as bedding in the dog house, however wood shavings (with as much dust as possible shaken out) greatly facilitate the cleaning of the outside dog areas. A large flat rock or small areas of patio stones seem to be appreciated by the dogs as a place to lie down.

147

The Kennel

NOISE

Whatever dogs you choose to keep, without regard to their socialization, they will bark or howl from time to time. **Most municipalities have legislated the number of dogs you may keep (usually 3).** The acceptable sound level within the limits of your property is often limited to 75 decibels. I have measured the sound levels from a variety of sources so that you can compare them. Clearly, these are average values which may vary according to the breed of dog, the humidity level, the air temperature, the nature of the environment, etc. It should also be remembered that the intensity of the sound is measured logarithmically (for example, 3 dogs will create a sound scarcely louder than one dog).

Some veterinarians are willing to operate on vocal cords, but I am totally opposed to this type of mutilation. Electric shock collars, triggered by barking, are neither efficient, nor recommended.

One of my friends has found a solution which merits consideration. **He has built a totally enclosed kennel.** No more problems with noise, freezing, rain, snow, wind, sun or skunks, etc. This may be the kennel of the future. He has even installed automatic water, feeding and cleaning systems, perhaps more costly, but definitely more practical. It is a fallacy to believe that dogs who do not live continually outdoors have less dense fur.

My kennel (± 35 Siberian Huskies) is located about half a mile from houses (Chenil Zéro, 2 Montée des Cèdres, St-Louis-de-Gonzague, Québec, Canada, JOS 1TO, 450-373-2655).

The Kennel

TYPICAL SOUND LEVELS

SOURCE   ## DECIBELS (dB)

SOURCE	DECIBELS (dB)	
1 husky ± 45 lbs	75	*
10 huskies ± 45 lbs	80	*
Car at 20km/hr.	70	*
Car at 60km/hr.	80	*
Normal conversation	70	
Movie theater	80	
Discotech	90	
Library	40	
Lawn mower	75	*
Snowmobile	80	*
Airplane	100	
Train locomotive	90	*

*measured at 30 feet from
the source of the sound.

Zamouray

Nome, Alaska, March 1995

The Kennel

DOG HOUSE

I have visited kennels from one end of Canada and the United States to the other. It seems to me that one style of house is ideal.

The Main Qualities

The construction is simple, reasonably inexpensive and easy to repair.
The suggested dimensions are for a sled dog of about 50 lbs. However the opening can be modified to adapt to nearly all dogs.
The roof is removable making the cleaning and straw replacement tasks easy. A bowl may be on the inside until the dog is big enough to jump up on his house.
A roof membrane can be glued to the cover to extend life expectancy.
A removable floor allows cleaning, and even its easy replacement, if necessary.
A space under the house minimizes both rot and the infiltration of parasites.
A lining around the door made of hard wood prevents the dogs from gnawing around the opening.
The dog bowl (flat bottom to avoid the ice sticking to the bowl) must be recessed, which prevents the dog from playing with his bowl needlessly and from dumping it (mesh enclosure).

The Kennel

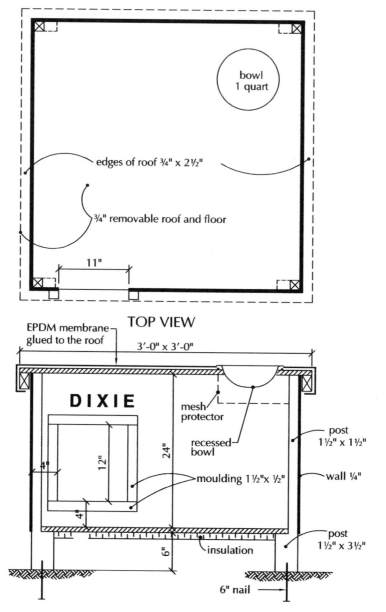

bowl
1 quart

edges of roof ¾" x 2½"

¾" removable roof and floor

11"

TOP VIEW

EPDM membrane glued to the roof

3'-0" x 3'-0"

DIXIE

mesh protector

recessed bowl

post 1½" x 1½"

12"

24"

4"

moulding 1½"x ½"

wall ¼"

4"

insulation

post 1½" x 3½"

6"

6" nail

FRONT VIEW

The Kennel

SLED DOG HOUSE

A stainless steel bowl allows easy cleaning and will last many years.
The shape of the bowl protects it from being mis-shapen by freezing and allows removal of ice in a couple of seconds in the winter. A mesh protector allows it to stay in place.
Dogs love wooden houses and these have proven to be very comfortable in winter. Sled dogs love to sit on their houses and a flat roof makes it easy for them to do so.
The edge of the removable roof, which extends beyond the walls, prevents water getting into the walls and rotting them.
The location of the door compared to the depth of the house keeps the straw in place and keeps it much cleaner than if the floor was at ground level.
The small opening is enough to allow adequate ventilation while limiting the entry of cold air during the winter.
The insulated floor makes it more comfortable during cold temperatures.
The nails under the legs of the doghouse prevent it from moving when a dog jumps on its house.
This type of house is light and very easily moved to another spot.

The Kennel

Moreover, dogs love to perch on their houses. This may allow them a better vision or it gives them greater comfort than lying on the ground. One thing is clear, that this encourages their agility and helps keep them in shape. To allow your dogs to jump up on their houses, they must be solid, otherwise, they will not feel secure and will not try it again. To prevent all lateral movement when your dog jumps on his house, the frame must be extremely rigid. A facing of plywood gives this advantage.

Avoid using a metal roof which, although long lasting, is susceptible to injuring a dog during very cold temperatures. Some breeders place an additional opening opposite the door which they leave open in the summer. This certainly allows better ventilation during warm or hot spells. It is always preferred to have the opening facing south to capture the greatest amount of sunshine. This direction also protects the house opening from the full blast of arctic air.

If your dog house is on a soft surface, such as soft earth or sand, etc., you would be wise to put a 6 inch nail under each leg of the house to stabilize it. **Your dogs will feel much more secure if their house is well stabilized on the ground.** When you move a dog to another area in your yard, try to keep the same house for him. This will leave the dog much less disoriented.

I am usually content with applying two coats of wood preservative on the exterior of the houses. If you decide to paint them, they should be white to reflect the maximum of the sun's rays. EPDM is a very good membrane which can be glued to the roof to protect from rain.

154

The Kennel

MANURE COMPOSTER

Most commercial kennels have to recuperate and treat their dog waste, and even then the ground has to be disinfected with strong chemicals (agricultural lime, javex solution, etc.). You can buy different models of pooper scoopers, however it is so easy to make one with an old candy can or wine metal can. Screw it to a broken hockey stick.

Whatever your kennel size, disposing of excrement will be a problem you must address. As well, you will be participating in a kind of recycling. The Department of Geophysics of the University of Alaska has developed a technique of composting dog manure with success. It requires building two or three cylinders about 30 inches in diameter by 36 inches high using a metal screening with openings of 1 inch x 1 inch.

The recipe is simple. Mix about two parts of dog manure to one part of cut straw, cut up twigs, shredded leaves or grass from your lawnmower (in fact, with whatever source of carbon), and moisten it all to improve the development of bacteria. Preferably, your compost containers should be sheltered from rain storms, but have lots of sunlight, for the sun helps in the process. It is important that the cylinders be in a relatively open area so that air circulation can allow good oxygen entry. However, a waterproof cover would prevent the rain from washing away the mixture.

Microorganisms at work will cause a rapid increase in temperature, which must exceed the minimum required 140°F necessary for the reproduction of microorganisms. In a period of high bacteriological activity, your compost container should "smoke" (give off

The Kennel

a mist) especially in the morning. When the temperature drops, it will be time to re-mix the ingredients to
assure that all the biodegradable materials have re-
acted. It is enough to remove the metal screen cylinder
and to relocate it, then refill it, re-mixing the remainder
of the first fermentation. Depending on the outside
temperature, you may make four such re-mixes and wait
4 to 8 weeks before having some compost. I do not
think that it is suitable to use this for your vegetable
garden. However it is ideal for flowers and shrubs. For
additional information and details you can contact
Fairbanks Soil and Water District, 1760 Westwood Way,
Fairbanks, Alaska, 99701, USA, Tel. 907-479-6767.

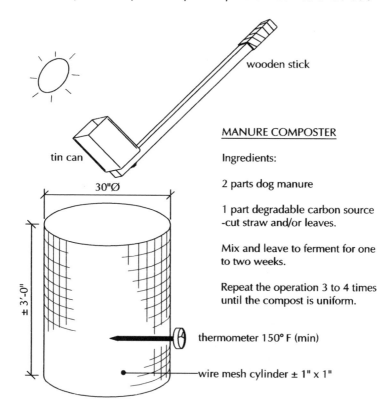

wooden stick

tin can

30"Ø

± 3'-0"

MANURE COMPOSTER

Ingredients:

2 parts dog manure

1 part degradable carbon source
-cut straw and/or leaves.

Mix and leave to ferment for one
to two weeks.

Repeat the operation 3 to 4 times
until the compost is uniform.

thermometer 150° F (min)

wire mesh cylinder ± 1" x 1"

Collars

Three collar styles are generally used for sled dogs. Made of nylon webbing, 1/8 inch thick and 1 inch wide, adjustable to allow fitting, and with a large ring for ease of connecting, these inexpensive collars should be used by all mushers. One musher explained to me that the colour of the collar on each dog corresponds to the colour code on the harness. Consequently he loses little time selecting the right harness for each dog when hooking up a team. A good idea is to keep some of them always available in your sled, your kennel or in your trailer in case of emergencies. It is extremely difficult to get ahold of a sled dog which has broken his collar.

Metal obedience collars (choke chains) are completely discouraged. It brings irreparable damage to the spirit of the dog.

Some dogs are specialists in getting out of their collars. Normally, when I can put two fingers easily between the dog's neck and its collar, the collar is tight enough. However, in exceptional cases, I use a semi-choke style which will close more snugly around the neck if excessive tension is put on it. During the winter, I frequently check collars and move them regularly to let the fur on the neck grow back. During the cold season I expand them a little to give space for the more dense winter coat.

standard collar
ring out

standard collar
ring in (reduces the risk of
the tongue freezing when
touching the ring)

semi-choke collar

Harnesses

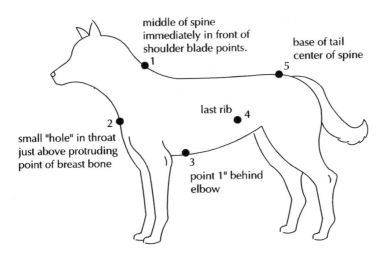

middle of spine immediately in front of shoulder blade points.

base of tail center of spine

last rib 4

small "hole" in throat just above protruding point of breast bone

point 1" behind elbow

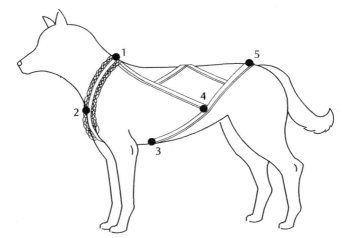

FITTING POINTS FOR HARNESS

Harnesses

A large variety of harnesses exist for sled dogs. They are usually made of polypropylene webbing, 0.03 inch thick and about 1 inch wide, in a variety of colors. Various materials are used as padding to spread the pressure on the front and chest of the dog. The size of the harness clearly must match the size of the dog. The colour of the tug cord usually indicates the harness size (small, medium, large, extra large, etc.) Also, it is very important that the harness ends at the beginning of the dog's tail. Most harnesses are not adjustable. A harness which is too large or too small will interfere with the dog's movement and increase the risk of injuries. Many dogs like their harnesses so much that they will eat them if the musher turns his back. To discourage this practice I have used Tabasco sauce with some success.

After use, the harness must be dried, checked and, if needed, repaired. Harnesses usually can be washed in a washing machine without shrinkage. Personally, I replace the regular tug cords with elastic ones. This reduces the shock. Some mushers add a fluorescent (reflective) tape on the back of the harness so they will be able to see their dogs better at night. The new "H" type (elastic) harness have just appeared on the market. I have tried them and found them to be less durable.

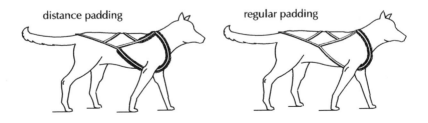

distance padding   regular padding

EQUIPMENT

Stake-out lines

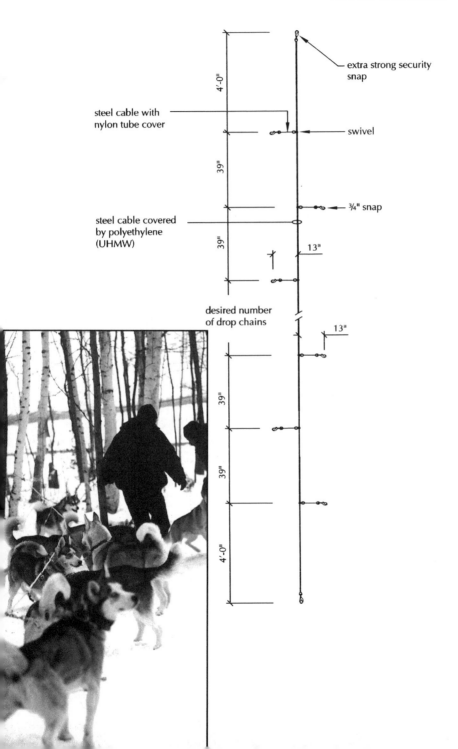

extra strong security snap

4'-0"

steel cable with nylon tube cover

swivel

39"

¾" snap

steel cable covered by polyethylene (UHMW)

39"

13"

desired number of drop chains

13"

39"

39"

4'-0"

Stake-out lines

When on a trip, you must be able to depend on a stake out line which is both light and, above all, absolutely reliable. It appears easy to use a chain (very heavy) or a steel cable (airline cable, difficult for making connections) with short pieces running off it, equipped with snaps. In using it you will note that the dogs cannot free themselves easily enough from this type of line. The connecting lines always end up wrapping around the main cable and the snaps then open. Invest now in a stake out line with the following characteristics:

1 - Main steel cable, 3/16 inch in diameter, flexible and covered with a polyethylene coating (VHMW).

2 - Short steel cable lines, 1/8 inch in diameter, covered with nylon, connected to the mainline on a swivel, with a snap at the other end.

3 - An extra strong snap at each end of the main line.

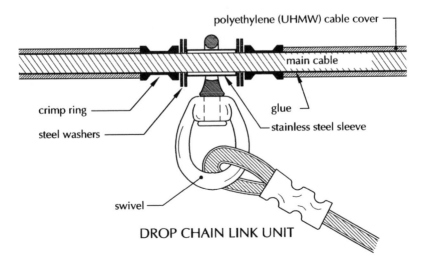

DROP CHAIN LINK UNIT

Ganglines

There are a variety of ways to hook up a dog team, each with its strengths and weaknesses.

FAN HITCH

The Inuit who travel in the Arctic tundra, without obstacles, on snow hard packed by winds, can use this style of hitch.

Its principal advantage is that each dog chooses its own track and can run a clear path in front of him. However, given that he exerts a pull which comes off the sled at an angle, the pulling force is slightly reduced. This type of hook-up clearly avoids the lines tangling. However, it favours contacts between dogs, often with disastrous consequences.

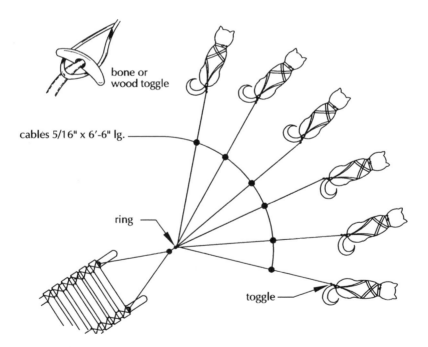

bone or wood toggle

cables 5/16" x 6'-6" lg.

ring

toggle

Ganglines

SINGLE LINE HITCH

This style of hook-up is used for travelling on very narrow trails such as trappers' trails to avoid two dogs being caught around a tree. It makes travelling easier in areas of uneven land or in very deep snow that the musher must pack with snowshoes ahead of the dogs. However, to my knowledge, only trappers use this style and I think its use must be limited to a maximum of six dogs. It is clearly easier to direct a team with a lead dog than with the group concept of the fan hitch. I own a complete hook-up of this style, but I use it only in public demonstrations. It is not only more complicated, but given that the dogs are not connected to a neckline, the least distraction of one of the dogs affects the team.

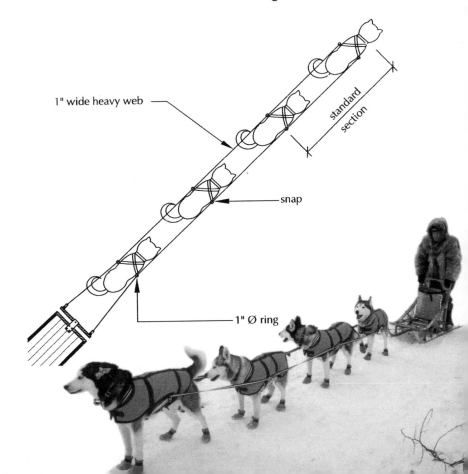

1" wide heavy web

standard section

snap

1" Ø ring

Ganglines

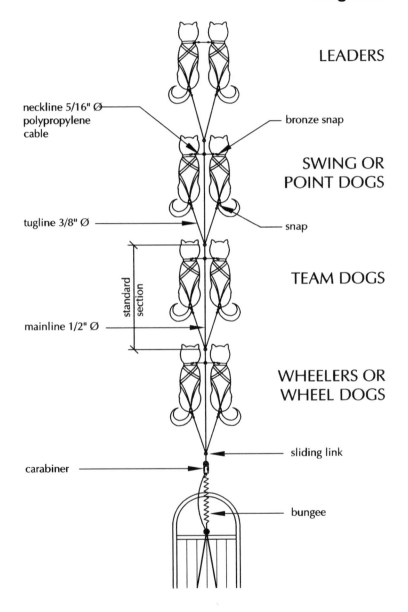

LEADERS

neckline 5/16" Ø
polypropylene
cable

bronze snap

SWING OR
POINT DOGS

tugline 3/8" Ø

snap

standard section

TEAM DOGS

mainline 1/2" Ø

WHEELERS OR
WHEEL DOGS

sliding link

carabiner

bungee

TANDEM HITCH

Ganglines

TANDEM HITCH

By far, the tandem hitch is the one most often used. Each dog is attached to the main line, both front and back, except lead dogs which are simply connected to each other by their collars. Often, mushers will use only one lead dog, or a dog may run alone elsewhere in the team. In this last case, the two tug lines are both connected to this dog's harness. Using two lead dogs reduces the stress since each dog feels less responsible for the pack. It also allows the driver to train a young dog with a more experienced dog. When a command is given, it is often better responded to when two are attentive to responding. If one makes a mistake, the other is there to correct him.

Most mushers have chosen this type of hitch. It helps keep some order among the dogs, dependent upon the lead dog keeping the line taut. The driver must use the brake to keep the line connecting the sled to the lead dogs always taut. This is not as easy as one might imagine. To keep the line taut the driver can also plant his heels on the snow to slow down the sled, while leaving the rest of his foot on the runner. This way it is easier to keep one's balance. On a trail that is somewhat uneven and with deep snow, some mushers detach the neckline from each of the dogs to allow them to work more freely. When I stop for a short rest I often detach the tugline from the dogs who are the most eager to start again.

Ganglines

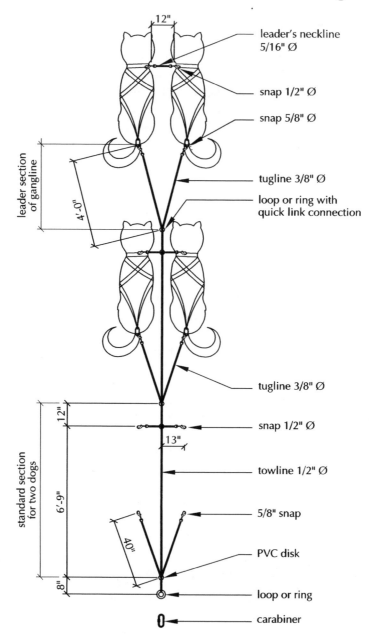

12"

leader's neckline
5/16" Ø

snap 1/2" Ø

snap 5/8" Ø

leader section
of gangline

4'-0"

tugline 3/8" Ø

loop or ring with
quick link connection

tugline 3/8" Ø

12"

snap 1/2" Ø

13"

standard section
for two dogs

6'-9"

towline 1/2" Ø

5/8" snap

40"

PVC disk

8"

loop or ring

carabiner

Ganglines

There are two kinds of ganglines, each with its strengths and weaknesses.

Polypropylene Gangline

This gangline is made up of a main line (towline) of ½ inch diameter braided polypropylene rope to which are connected to the tuglines and necklines of 5/16 inch diameter rope. These ropes are usually made of 12 strands and come in different colours, which helps when sorting out a tangle. Each section (two dogs are in a section) is independent, which allows easy changes in the line if the number of dogs in the team increases or decreases. The measurements of the lines vary as a function of the length of the dogs and depending on the type of activity. All parts usually are detachable for ease of replacing a snap or a line. It is essential that you buy a fid (a tool for braiding these ropes) for each size of rope so that you will be able to modify or repair your lines.

Cable (Steel cable covered with plastic) Gangline

To deal with a bad habit of some sled dogs which eat the lines, a stainless steel cable, 1/8 inch in diametre, has been put in a nylon sheath and is used as the main line (towline) as well as the necklines attaching the dog from his collar to the main line. The tuglines remain polypropylene rope 3/8 inch in diametre. This assembly is put together with a rotating disk and quick links of 1/4 inch in diametre. As in the previous situation, these lines are made in two dog sections and are connected to each other by a locking link. Although heavier, these lines are much stronger, and resist the effect of dogs chewing lines.

Ganglines

If you plan to rest your dogs for long periods of time leaving them in the lines, I suggest that you detach the front line. This gives them much more space. In this case, the space between two dogs must be larger to prevent the dogs reaching the two behind them and getting their lines tangled.

It is also recommended that the main line be made of steel cable, without which you may find yourself with a few less dogs.

To avoid injuries, the neckline snap must be somewhat weak (½ inch diametre) so that it will break if an obstacle (tree, stump, etc.) comes between the dog and the main line.

You can buy such lines at most specialized stores. However, sooner or later, you will have to repair or modify them to accommodate certain dogs. If you have a little time available I recommend that you make them yourself. This is quite easy and, in addition, you will develop an ability to accomplish the eventually necessary repairs. I dip my snaps in water repellent oil which minimize freezing but I always carry with me a lock de-icer spray.

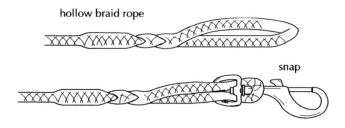

hollow braid rope

snap

Ganglines

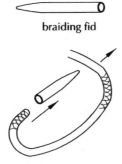
braiding fid

hollow braid rope

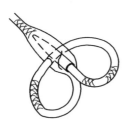

or

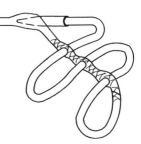

USING A FID

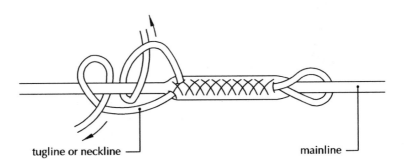

tugline or neckline ——

mainline ——

GANGLINE

Toboggan style sled

Basket style sled

Sleds

I have been on muskox hunting trips using Inuit sleds measuring 4 feet wide and 8 feet long. I have also tried the flexible aluminum sleds built by the Europeans. Those who are racing need sleds that are light weight and highly manoeuverable. Amateurs doing expeditions need large and very stable sleds. The majority of mushers in between need good solid and adaptable sleds.

Building your own sled for your first is not the best idea. Someone starting out in the sport is better to try out different models so that a choice as to model type can be based on meeting individual needs and preferences. A steel sled is very solid, but very heavy. Aluminum sleds are lighter, but have less flexibility. Sleds made out of plastic components are practically indestructible except in extremely cold temperatures or if the sled has been left outside in the sun for extended periods of time. (Exposure over time to the sun will weaken the molecular structure of plastic). Plastic sleds are also difficult to repair. **Wood remains the most popular substance for making sleds.** When all necessary functions of a sled are considered, wood is the most efficient. It is light, flexible, easily shaped, durable, simple to repair and above all, still captures the majesty of the history of dog sledding. White oak as a dense and hard wood is most commonly used. It is easy to bend and very resistant to deterioration. Walnut, birch, ash, and maple are also used. Covering the handle bar of the sled with a foam insulating sleeve (the type used to cover pipes) is a good idea. You will find this much warmer for your hands. For other associated equipment needed, try to maintain compatibility by staying with the same manufacturer (e.g. **AKKO,** Box 977, Hudson, Québec JOP 1HO, Tel.(450) 458-5910.

Sleds

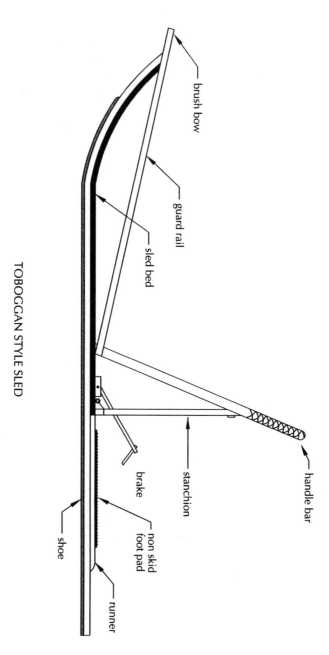

TOBOGGAN STYLE SLED

brush bow

guard rail

sled bed

brake

stanchion

non skid
foot pad

shoe

runner

handle bar

Sleds

I have never seen two sleds exactly alike. Even if two mushers have bought two similar sleds from the same manufacturer, they will vary the modifications and options added to suit their own preferences. I have even seen a fold-down ultra-lite sled created by an Alaskan musher. In effect, your own sled must be one that will respond to the type of sledding that you do with it. Never forget that the best spot to have a nap or to sleep overnight is in the basket of your sled. Be sure to put snow all around your sled, as the air cushion under the sled will serve as very good insulation. There are in fact two major types of sleds.

Basket Sleds

The main characteristic of these sleds is that the floor or bed of the sled is elevated ± 8 inches above the runners. This sled is used almost exclusively by short distance mushers (less than 20 miles). Flexibility, manoeuverability and light weight override the disadvantage of a higher center of gravity. It also offers little resistance to the wind and has good adherence to trail surfaces. It is a sled that is far easier to drive on mountainous trails than is the toboggan sled.

Toboggan Sleds

The floor or bed of this sled is just barely higher than the runners (plus/minus 3 inches). This is the sled that is usually used for expeditions for its capability of carrying loads of 1000 pounds or more over many different surfaces (e.g. deep snow). The number of dogs used to haul these big loads will vary from twelve to twenty-two. The low center of gravity reduces the likelihood of tipping, but they necessitate more maintenance. The underneath must be treated almost every

Sleds

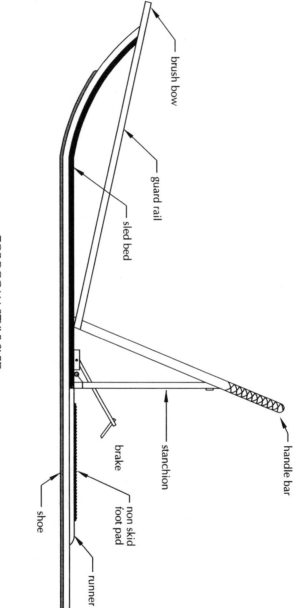

brush bow

guard rail

sled bed

TOBOGGAN STYLE SLED

brake

stanchion

handle bar

shoe

non skid
foot pad

runner

174

Sleds

year, due to friction. Even if the sled hits an obstacle, it will bounce back in the right direction.

A ring located at the center of the sled concentrates the lines, centering the force and keeping lines above the ground (plus/minus 12 inches). It is also this ring which helps the sled navigate turns. The pulling lines are simply passed through this ring without being tied in place because the sled structure is too fragile.

After passing through this ring from the front, the line must separate so as to attach directly, one to each runner, preferably on a plate to distribute the pull. In this way the tension is directly applied to the runners, avoiding structural problems. The anchors, brakes and safety line (snubline for starts) are also directly attached to the runners, being the points for distributing tension.

The structure of some sleds does not allow such a set-up (e.g. toboggan sled, single central brake). If some concept is important, it is that the tension must come from the runners. In the same way, the brakes, snow hooks and safety line must also be attached to the runners, at the same points if possible.

I have attached to the end of each of the runners eyelets to tow another sled or a small toboggan. I have also towed a snowmobile on two occasions. A dog is able to provide a continuous tension almost equal to a quarter of his weight. However, at the start, when the dogs are especially excited, this force may easily be doubled or tripled, so imagine multiplying this by the number of dogs. It is easy to understand the importance of ways of attaching all the tension cables at the same point on each side of the sled.

Sleds

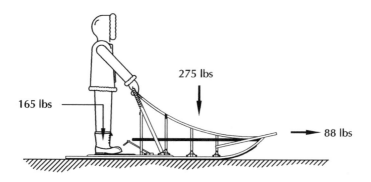

275 lbs

165 lbs

88 lbs

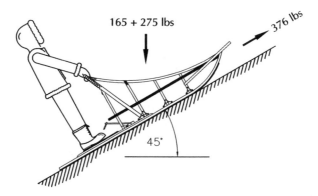

165 + 275 lbs

376 lbs

45°

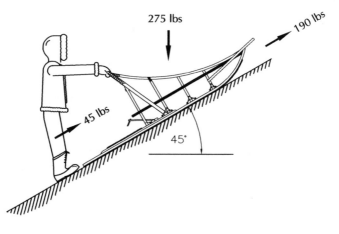

275 lbs

190 lbs

45 lbs

45°

Sleds

How much weight is a sled dog able to pull? How much force is needed to pull a sled? Simple questions, but questions requiring complex answers. Generally, a well trained sled dog should be able to pull the equivalent of his weight over an extended period of time. This of course will depend on a number of variables : i.e. the condition of the sled and runners, the type of snow, or the type of terrain. Answering the second question is equally complex. The required force of pulling will vary according to the snow type, runners used, the temperature, the weight of the sled, etc. It is possible to evaluate the difference between the force required to pull a sled on a level surface or on an incline. This in turn will clearly show the importance for the musher to help his team by removing himself as a passenger and helping by pushing the sled when climbing a hill.

The first example shows a musher weighing 165 pounds standing on the runners of a sled. The sled and baggage weigh 275 pounds. Snow conditions add a coefficient of friction of 0.02. Using the principles of physics, one is able to calculate that a dog team pulling a load of the above parameters on a level surface will be required to furnish pulling power of approximately 88 pounds. On an incline of 45 degrees however, the coefficient of friction reduces slightly due to the shift in gravitational influence. Maintaining other variables the same, the pulling power now required will be in the range of 376 pounds. This is more than four times that required on the level! If the musher helps his team by disembarking the sled and assisting by pushing at a force of 45 pounds, then the pulling power required by the dogs will be reduced to 190 pounds. **This is one-half of the amount of force required than if the musher stays on the sled as a passenger and doesn't help by pushing.**

Sleds

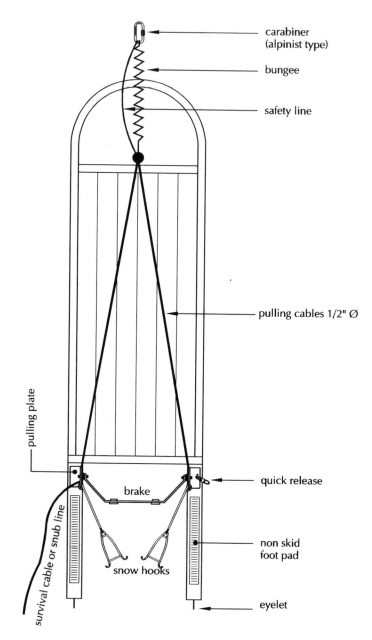

- carabiner (alpinist type)
- bungee
- safety line
- pulling cables 1/2" Ø
- pulling plate
- quick release
- brake
- survival cable or snub line
- non skid foot pad
- snow hooks
- eyelet

Sleds

BUNGEE CORDS

Before the start when the dogs are particularly eager to leave or when traveling or if the sled gets blocked by an obstacle, the force on the lines that pull the sled may greatly exceed their capacity or that of the connections to the sled. To reduce this overload, a bungee cord is put between the main gangline and the sled. This will balance the force between the sled and the dogs. The bungee is always put in place with a matching security line a little shorter than the full extension of the bungee, in case the bungee breaks, leading to a loose team. Some mushers also put a smaller bungee at the back of each dog's harness.

The ring at the end of the bungee is also an ideal place to put some spare parts. In this way you will always have some easily at hand in an emergency. I usually put two snaps and two quick links there. If you use very narrow trails, it isn't a bad idea to have the last two dogs attached directly to the sled, without their tug lines going to the mainline. First, the force to the sled will be slightly increased (plus/minus 3 to 5%) because the dog will be pulling in a straight line, not at an angle. Secondly, this line attachment may help you to more easily get around trees and to protect somewhat the brush bow of your sled. The dog's tuglines should have a bungee to avoid the effect of too great a force onto the shoulders of the dog. Your sled needs to be adapted to allow this type of hook up.

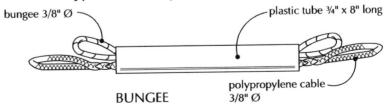

bungee 3/8" Ø

plastic tube ¾" x 8" long

polypropylene cable 3/8" Ø

BUNGEE

Sleds

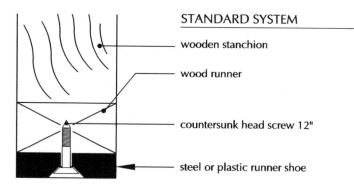

STANDARD SYSTEM

wooden stanchion

wood runner

countersunk head screw 12"

steel or plastic runner shoe

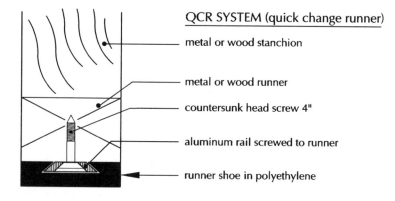

QCR SYSTEM (quick change runner)

metal or wood stanchion

metal or wood runner

countersunk head screw 4"

aluminum rail screwed to runner

runner shoe in polyethylene

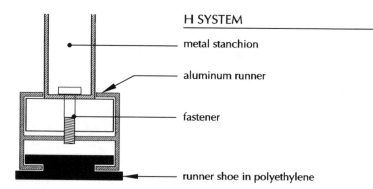

H SYSTEM

metal stanchion

aluminum runner

fastener

runner shoe in polyethylene

Sleds

RUNNERS AND SHOES

Whatever type of activities you plan, the choice of runner shoes is an important one. There is a great variety of shoes, in hardwood, plastic or metal. There is nothing better than the QCR (Quick Change Runner) system. It consists of a metal rail which forms an inverted V. This allows one to easily slide on and off plastic shoes, prepared with the appropriate groove to fit the rail. At the end of each season, I always remove these shoes so that the wood of the runner can easily dry. These sleds are expensive, so it is important to pay attention to their maintenance.

The installation of the rail is made with close fitting, counter-sunk screws. With the help of a lubricant, if necessary, the plastic shoe slides onto this rail. Two small bolts are then used at the front of the runner, through the plastic and the rail, to keep everything in place. The main advantage of this system is in the ease of changing runner shoes, either to put on a more appropriate plastic for the conditions or to replace damaged shoes. It is important to note that with this system there are no openings under the shoe (i.e. on the snow surface). Other forms of mounting plastic shoes require holes for the screws and it is almost impossible to guarantee that they will remain covered (e.g. with wax), thereby increasing the friction.

The width of the shoes is usually determined by the width of the runners, which are usually made of wood. It is necessary that the plastic shoes be at least as wide as the wood runner, which must be protected from obstacles. Plastic shoes are available in widths of 1½ inches, 2 inches and 2½ inches and in thicknesses of 3/8 inch and ½ inch. On a hard surface a narrow runner glides better; on a soft surface, however, the narrow runner will sink and increase the drag. The type of plastic also has a significant effect on the drag. UHMW or UH4000 (**Ultra High Molecular Weight-polyethylene**) are both very resistant and slick. **P-Tex®** is also slick. It is less resistant, but easily repaired with hot wax, as are skis. The temperature also affects the drag, depending on the type of plastic used.

When putting on the runner shoes I suggest you lubricate them with **Pledge®** furniture polish. It is surprising how this helps the plastics slide onto the rails easily, even in sub-zero temperatures.

Other types of shoes are also available, obviously at a lower price. If you foresee beginning training in very difficult conditions, you might consider equipping one of your sleds with very hard and resistant plastic or with hard metal (steel). If, however your trips are limited, simple plastic shoes, screwed on with counter-sunk screws will also be a good investment.

Some mushers are actually trying to develop a runner of aluminum in the shape of an H, which would allow the installation of interchangeable plastic under it. Special connectors permit installation to allow the basket to slide the length of the sled. The Inuit often use runners of green wood (birch) which they simply cover with ice or frozen urine. A sled should never be left on the snow overnight because snow will stick to the shoes. It should be tilted on its side or up against a wall.

Sleds

CHARACTERISTICS OF THE VARIOUS MATERIALS
USED AS RUNNER SHOES

UHMW **and** **UH-4000**	Polyethylene, resistant, inexpensive, available in a variety of sizes, used for runner shoes and toboggans.
P-TEX 2000 **and** **HM 3**	Polyethylene, very popular for speed races. Mushers glue it to the runners (**contact cement 3M®**). The coefficient of friction is very low when treated with hot wax. However, it is not very hard or resistent.
HX **and** **HD**	Polyethylene, used for races run in very low temperatures, affordable cost but it wears out quickly.
ORANGE V	Polyethylene, expensive, but very resistant whatever the temperature may be. It can be used on earth or sand.
TEFLON	Coefficient of friction is very low but has little resistance (hardness) and is quite expensive.
STEEL	Very durable, even in the worst conditions, lessens skidding, but is heavy and has a lot of friction.
WOOD	The Inuit sometimes use runners of birch wood.

*   Most plastics are affected by sunlight.

TROTTINETTES (KICK SLEDS)

Scandinavians did not take long to change this sport into a method of transport adapted to their daily lives. They have developed a very light sled which can be easily pulled by one, two or three dogs, or pushed by someone, as one would pedal a scooter. These sleds are very light, easily handled and not too expensive. Clearly, **this toy cannot be compared to a conventional sled**, and even less replace it, mainly because of poor stability and of the absence of an efficient braking system.

Buffy, Dixie and Bernard

Sleds

DRAG

Regardless of the type of runner shoes used, friction will be determined by the following factors :

* The density of the snow at the front of the runners will determine the degree to which the runners will sink into the snow. This, clearly, will bring about resistance of varying degrees. If the snow is too deep it may even pile up in front of your sled and considerably increase the resistance. It is this type of situation in which the toboggan type of sled is preferred.

* Depending upon the temperature of the snow, the thermal conductivity of the runner shoes, as well as its pressure on the snow, the first section of each runner shoe will slide directly on ice crystals. This section of the shoes must have a particularly hard quality, because this type of friction (dry) is the same as if the sled was sliding on sand. When the outside temperature is below - 40°F, this type of friction occurs on the full length of the runner shoes.

* If the air temperature is high, the temperature under the shoes will increase (because of the friction) until a thin layer of water forms between the shoes and the snow. This layer of water acts as a lubricant which considerably lowers the friction on this section of the shoes.

* Along with other factors, the layer of water gradually increases along the length of runners until it is great enough to increase the capillary tension, which increases the drag and finally creates great resistance for the last section of the shoes.

Sleds

* The friction between the runner shoes and the snow also creates a magnetic field which attracts dust which sticks to the shoes. These dust-like pieces make the surface rough and, consequently, increase the friction.

From these observations it is easy to understand that the total friction is less on hard snow, with shoes having a weak thermal conductivity and a smooth and hard surface, all occurring in moderate temperatures, between 23°F and - 4°F. The two runners clearly must be perfectly parallel and the pulling point exactly in the centre. If your tracks in the snow are wider than your runner shoes, it is clear you have a problem with alignment.

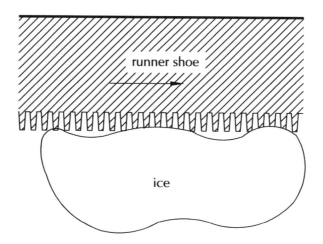

When the temperature is above - 22°F, polyethylene has an excellent coefficient of friction. It provides a surface which is harder than ice however its elasticity allows it to minimize the friction on ice particles.

Sleds

The polyethylene shoes adjust like elastic when going over ice, bringing about water creation at the top and re-crystallization of snow in the tips, which finally increases its straight surface.

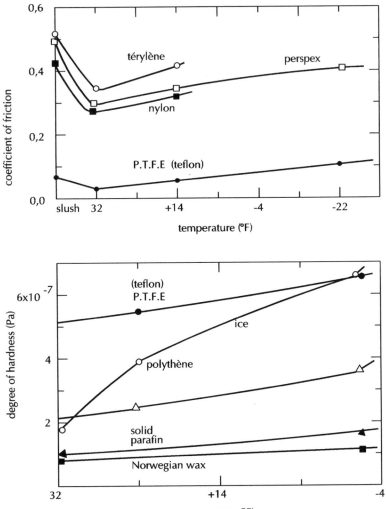

Sleds

Using appropriate wax for the temperature also reduces the roughness of the shoes and consequently the friction. This is especially important when the temperatures are very low and the friction comes from dry snow. If you want to know more on this subject, I suggest you read the study done by the U.S. Army Corps of Engineers, Monograph 92-2, "A REVIEW OF THE PROCESSES THAT CONTROL SNOW FRICTION", **Samuel C. Colbeck**, April 92, usually available at university libraries. Loading the weight somewhat toward the rear of the sled will allow the sled to swivel and steer more easily.

BRAKES

The brake is one of the most important pieces of any dog sled. The musher has to use his brake often. In fact, the main problem for the musher is to make sure that the mainline (towline) which connects the sled to the lead dogs is taut, to avoid the dogs becoming tangled in the lines. Frequently, espacally at the start, the other dogs want to run faster than the lead dogs. The brake must also be used to slow down in turns or even to stop the team. When the musher gives the command to stop - 'WHOA' - he brakes at the same time to let the dogs know he wants to stop. It is important that the brake slide a bit on the surface, not like the snow hook (**totally stopping the sled instantly**), otherwise this might break the sled and injure the driver and any passengers. The contact point must also be very strong (carbide points). The total assembly must also be very strong and its application very simple because the brake must often be used in emergencies.

Sleds

SINGLE BRAKE

This brake is simpler, but less efficient. It is often used on small sleds, pulled by only a few dogs. Less costly and easy to make, nonetheless it is not very resistant or effective.

SNOWMOBILE TREAD BRAKE

Many mushers use a section of a snowmobile tread or belt as a brake. Some have added carbide points to increase its efficiency. Its main advantage without a doubt is its comfort. The musher can usually stand on it to slow down the sled, this can be done without stopping the sled. Some of these are even detachable, but in most cases, another type of brake is required to stop the sled. This brake damages the trail less, but is much more awkward.

Sleds

STANDARD BRAKE

This is by far the most common and most efficient brake. It comes in various models, more or less sophisticated. Its construction seems simple, however it is recommended that you buy one from a well-known manufacturer. The pivots must be functional, the carbide tips very resistant and the construction both strong and light. This style of brake is expensive, but worth it. One musher has put a rubber cover on the push bar. This seemed to me a good idea.

HANDLE COVER

Donna with her muskrat muff

When on long trips, the musher is constantly holding the driving bow of the sled. He must also, from time to time, take his hands out to do one thing or another. In very cold temperatures his hands are, naturally, vulnerable to frostbite, so I have made a muff of muskrat fur which keeps my hands warm even when wearing light gloves. It has also been helpful to add a small pocket where I put sunglasses, a compass, a pocket flashlight, a lighter, brass wire, etc.

Sleds

SNUB LINE / SAFETY ROPE

When one is hooking up a dog team, the sled must be securely tied, since the dogs are always eager to go. Using a quick release is essential, since it is almost impossible to undo a snap to release the team. There are two main types of quick releases.

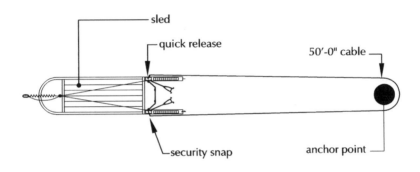

Personally, I don't have great confidence in the sliding type, and even if I use the largest marine quality model, I divide the tension in two, returning it to the sled. When I release the quick release, the snubline which holds the sled goes around the holding post and trails behind the sled. If, by chance, a bad manoeuver leads me to fall off the sled, I am able to grab this line to attempt to stop the sled. This trailing snubline is also very usefull to attach my sled to trees along the trails. Be sure your line does not get hung up on something while you travel. Certainly, leave slowly with the brake on until the snubline has come around its post. This avoids some undesirable surprises.

EQUIPMENT

Sleds

I usually leave the line trailing until the dogs have reached their cruising speed. I must add, however, that before the start I almost always attach a security line to the collar of one of my lead dogs, which I take off at the last moment. This practice has served me well at least twice when my quick release was broken. Unfortunately, these two quick releases tend to freeze up. I know some mushers who will not take the risk of using them. They tie their main line to a tree and hook up their lead dogs last.

Some mushers use their snub line only, without a quick release. They take the line around a tree or something similar, then connect the line, as previously, with a buckle which they are able to undo while on the sled. This is particularly effective if the line is large enough and the connecting point is close enough to the sled.

LEASH

Because we know our dogs well, we usually move them by taking them by the collar. However, a leash made of a large rope (1 inch in diameter) or nylon webbing (1/8 inch thick by 1 inch wide) around 10 feet long, should be part of the equipment of every dog sled. This leash can be used to attach a wounded dog in your sled. This leash is also especially helpful in emergency situations or when people who are less experienced are asked to help with the dogs. In these situations, the dogs themselves are more at ease at the end of a leash than when directly handled by a stranger. Personally, I have leashes everywhere, quickly available and it has been very helpful.

EQUIPMENT

BAG

A waterproof bag is practically indispensable on all expedition sleds. Even in short races, most promoters (races or expeditions) require that a bag be available in which to put an injured dog. I suggest that you do not skimp on the size or the quality of the bag. Use a material which tolerates the cold as well as dog bites, preferably also flexible. Do not forget to have compartments built in to store small accessories close at hand. I suggest a wrap around closure which is adjustable to the amount of stock in your sled. If it is a zipper closure it must be particularly durable and must tolerate very cold temperatures.

Plan the fashion of tying it in the sled so that it will stay in place, even if the sled turns completely upside down.

Design it to be large enough for yourself, in the event you might have to spend the night in it. Before packing it, I put in a small waterproof mattress around 1 inch thick. This limits the rubbing between the baggage and the sled bed which could damage the bag. This mattress is also practical for sleeping. Always put it inside the bag until you are ready to use it, otherwise you will have to suffer with the ice which is likely to form on it.

Small compartments, easily accessible when you are standing at the back of the sled, are also very practical. Because of this I have easily at hand some double snaps for emergencies, a pair of pliers, a pair of gloves, a small knife, a lighter, a flashlight, a whistle to stop dog fights or to announce my presence in emergencies, a pair of binoculars, hand warmers, etc.

Sleds

SEAT

Some mushers have installed retractable seats at the back of their sleds. Certainly these are useful for long distance trips. To do this they use a bicycle seat mounted on an axis equipped with two hinges.

FOOTPADS

It can be difficult to keep standing on the runners when they become icy. Many types of rubber, however, can be used as a non-skid surface. It seems that the best solution is to cut strips from an old tire inner tube and to staple them in a looping (accordion) fashion on the runners.

Sleds

A SECONDARY TOBOGGAN

If you plan an expedition, even if it is for a few days, it is essential to have a plastic toboggan. At the end of the day you will find it practical to transport water or your luggage to the chalet. I use this toboggan also for feeding the dogs and cleaning up the kennel. I have fixed two eye bolts at the back of my sled runners to pull the toboggan. This is very practical because I can use it to carry light items (sleeping bags, changes of clothing, etc.) and to save space on my sled.

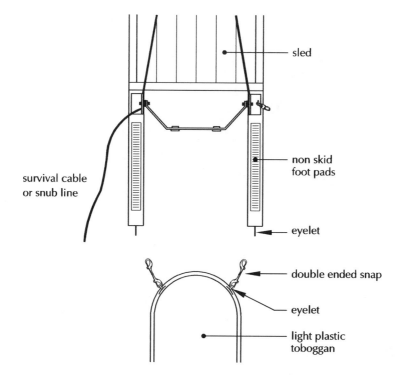

sled

non skid
foot pads

survival cable
or snub line

eyelet

double ended snap

eyelet

light plastic
toboggan

Other accessories

SNOW HOOKS

Two types of snow hooks are mainly used.

HOOK

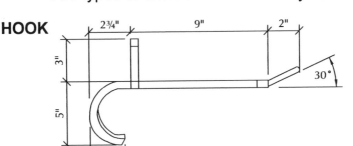

Made of steel reinforcing rods (½ inch x ½ inch) these are by far the most used. Holders made of PVC are available to carry them at the back of the sled. Many mushers carry two. This type of hook anchor always requires well packed snow and has frequently proven inadequate in southern Québec. This hook can also be used to hook to a tree. The rope holding the hook must be a length which allows the musher to remove it easily while standing at the back of the sled, in order to leave. A very strong security snap must be used, because you have no room for a mistake. This type of hook can also be used to defend yourself against a bear or wild dog.

Other accessories

DANFOSS (BRUSH HOOK)

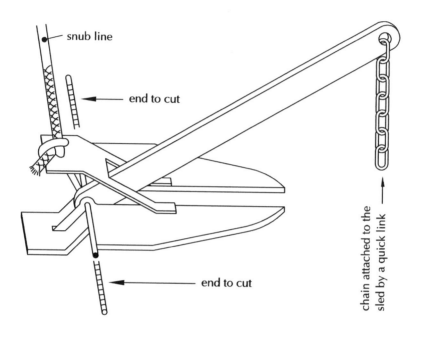

snub line

end to cut

end to cut

chain attached to the
sled by a quick link

A new type of anchor has begun to appear on the trails. In fact, this is a boat anchor, from which someone has simply cut off the two ends.

This type of anchor seems to be more effective in less dense snow. It is also much easier to pick up. Carrying it is easy, and its weight is comparable to other models. Using it around a tree or other object is also possible.

Other accessories

COATS

It may seem a little exaggerated to think of coats for your sled dogs, even so, just as we, they can be cold. Imagine an animal who runs dozens of miles and who stops abruptly in a temperature of -25°F. The harness compacts the fur. A little condensation has developed under the fur. It isn't difficult to understand. If you do not cover your dogs they will catch cold. Manufacturers offer a complete assortment of coats. I think that it is necessary, above all else, to consider simplicity and affordable cost. It is also necessary to understand that an injured dog, just as a human, has a tendency to shiver and must be protected from the cold by a coat or a blanket or even with auxiliary heat (such as. hand warmers). If the temperature drops severely, some dogs need a coat to protect their most exposed parts.

SNOWSHOES

There are still mushers who leave for a trip of many miles without snowshoes. They all have good reasons. It is nice out, the T.V. didn't forecast a snow-storm, I'll not be longer than two days, they are awkward to carry for nothing, etc. It is not even questionable. **One pair of snowshoes fitted with an adjustable boot harness that you carry must be on all sleds.** Dozens of events might occur. A good pair of snow-shoes weighs less than 5 pounds and can give you indispensable help. I use the Algonquin style made by the natives of Village Huron near Québec City. Take the time to try them out and train your lead dogs to follow you in the event that you have to open a new trail in deep snow.

Other accessories

DOG BOWLS

When on your dog trips I suggest you use flexible plastic dog bowls which are stackable and freeze proof. Some are specially made to be stable and they also have the advantage of keeping the food warm longer. I suggest you even keep one for yourself. It will warm your hands while you eat. Metal bowls are more durable, but the dogs may damage their tongues or muzzles, touching these bowls when they are very cold. To serve food or soup from a pot, I use an old granit saucepan on which I attach a long wooden handle (old hockey stick). This is so practical that most of my friends have copied it. Just as all utensils and cooking pots, the bowls must be washed regularly to prevent the development of bacteria which could spoil the food.

Donna feeding St-Louis

Other accessories

TOOLS

It is likely, if not certain, that one day or another you will have to face an unforeseen situation. Your sled may break on an obstacle. You may find a friend in trouble. You may try a bad trail and have to spend the night outdoors. Some things will then provide unexpected value (a corkscrew to open a bottle of wine).

More seriously, a simple fish hook will allow you to catch fish; some brass wire, to snare rabbits; a roll of duct tape to repair a sled, a multi-function tool, having knife, scissors, pliers, screwdrivers, wood saw, can opener, etc. will prove, without doubt, extremely practical. Of course you need an assortment of bolts, nuts and wood screws to repair your sled, your equipment or your dog harnesses. A small pocket flashlight will let you make repairs, particularly if your headlamp quits. Choose a medium size axe (18 to 24 inch handle) in case you have to cut your way through a large tree on the trail, build a shelter, or deal with a moose who refuses to let you have the trail. My friends who say they don't need such a tool, borrow mine constantly. I also always carry with me a double bolt swivel snap which helped me face all sorts or emergency situations (to replace a broken snap, to reduce or adjust a chain lenght, etc...)

Certainly, it is not a matter of overloading your sled by adding to your tools in case you might need them. It is enough to assure yourself that you have what you need to make necessary repairs. Your tools must also be easily accessible. In an emergency you don't have the time to unload your sled completely to find your axe.

Donna cooking dog food

Other accessories

PORTABLE STOVE

If you plan expeditions with your sled dogs, above all don't forget a portable stove. This stove must as much as possible, be able to heat the dogs' food, your food, and even yourself a little if you need it. Two types of stoves seem to me to be indispensable, each according to the type of trip you are planning. If the temperatures remain above -5°F, you use fewer than 10 dogs and you are not pressed for time, the naphtha stove will be your logical choice. The fuel is inexpensive, available in light containers and efficiently fuels both lamps and portable stoves. New appliances are also able to use ordinary unleaded gasoline. I recommend that you buy a small stove with two burners and a lamp with many extra mantles and a spare exterior globe.

ALCOHOL STOVE

On my last visit to Alaska at the time of the famous Iditarod Sled Dog Race, I was almost a rookie. Although I had read almost all the books on the subject, even raised sled dogs for 30 years, there in front of me were 58 mushers who all used the same type of portable stove, one I had never heard of. This type of stove was so superior that it was the only one allowed in this race of 1000 miles, crossing the state of Alaska. The race authorities even supply the fuel at each checkpoint.

It goes without saying that I was impressed by the demonstrations. In fact, it was so new that almost each musher had his or her own model. When I attended a number of other demonstrations, it was clear that this type of portable stove had not yet been sufficiently

Other accessories

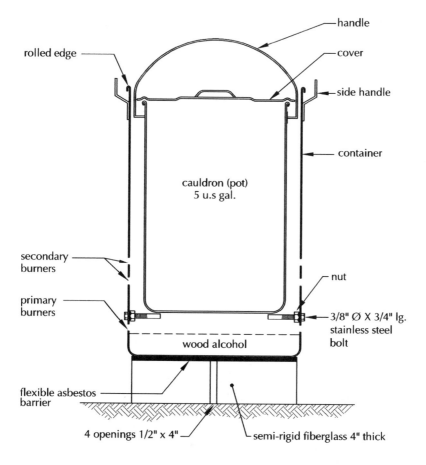

ALCOHOL STOVE

Other accessories

perfected. One of the craftsmen explained some of the advantages to me. Propane and naphtha are excellent fuels. However, both must be vaporized in order to burn. Propane containers are heavy and require a burner. Kerosene is dangerous to transport, and the burners require a pressurization which is difficult to achieve in temperatures below -5°F.

The portable alcohol stove is not dangerous and does not require any special parts. A 5 gallon boiler with burners at the bottom serves as a container for the fuel (around 2 quarts of alcohol). A piece of toilet paper (always available on well equipped sleds) provides e-nough flame to start the vaporization of alcohol, its combustion and even to keep it going in the arctic temperatures of Alaska. **The water in a 5 gallon container will be boiling 30 minutes later.** Incredible! No sophisticated burner, no pump, no dangerous fuel, no heavy container and even easy to light! This is really a jewel ! Extremely fast, lightweight, and practically free. Its only real drawback is the higher cost of the fuel.

The one which the Iditarod participants must use is a portable stove with a nominal capacity of 5 gallons. Normally, the racers prepare a meal for their 16 dogs, then while the dogs eat, they usually prepare a second serving which they keep hot in an insulated container which they give to their dogs 2-4 hours later.

Most of the mushers also cook their own meals on it, using of course a different pot. This set up also could be used as a wood burner with a grill to make a barbecue or just to boil water for a soup or coffee.

EQUIPMENT

Other accessories

In case you decide to make your own portable alcohol stove, it is very important that you completely understand its functioning.

* The interior boiler must have an exterior diameter of about 1 inch less than the exterior container. The interior boiler would ideally be positioned about 1 inch above the level of alcohol, which itself will vary between 0 and 1 inch. The tops of the two containers must be almost equal for the ease of mixing foods and to avoid wasting energy.

* The lowest burners must be located to avoid the fuel spilling when the ground is not perfectly level, and not too high, for it is these holes which brings the air close to the surface of the liquid which allows the evaporation of the alcohol. The rate of evaporation of the alcohol will depend on many factors such as the temperature of the liquid, the air temperature, the amount of air (dependent upon the size of the holes) as well as the distance between the air entrance and the level of the fuel. The holes must not be too large, since the wind will affect the combustion too much.

* The highest burners (holes) must allow the remaining alcohol vapour to burn before reaching the top of the boiler. Even if the evaporation conditions are ideal, no flame should reach above the lip of the boiler. One would think that one should increase the number of secondary burners. One should above all not forget that when the evaporation of the fuel will be at its lowest, if the ventilation is too great it will cool the pot. The secondary burners must also be put as low as possible to prevent the smoke from leaving by these openings. Not only would this reduce its efficiency, but even more, it would dirty the outside of the container.

Other accessories

* The outside container must have side handles. The inside pot should have a swing handle to facilitate drawing water or snow.

It is useless to tell you that I have had a lot of experience and that I have met many mushers who have each developed their own prototype. On paper, everything seems easy and available. When you attempt to assemble all the parts, you will encounter numerous difficulties. My first alcohol stove, a very simple one, was made with a 4 gallon container, a stainless steel colander as a support and a 2 gallon container as a boiler (pot). This system works very well, is light, costs almost nothing, but remains somewhat fragile. Given that I lose all sense of economy when it comes to my dogs, I also made another one, that with a commercial 4 gallon pot, a stainless steel container that I had made to measure with four stainless steel bolts, 3/8 inch dia x 3 inches long, to support the inside pot. This one is truly a jewel, but very heavy, and most of all, very expensive. It must be recognized that this type of water heater is used only on major outings or expeditions.

To prevent this apparatus from sinking into the snow, I created a fibreglass support on which I glued a flexible asbestos cloth. This cushion is also useful for travelling in the sled. I place it in the large container so that the bottom of the inside pot doesn't rub on the bolts.

Another small plastic bucket containing my mess kit (which also heats with alcohol) allows me to draw water, or snow to fill my pot. I also carry an asbestos mitt and a ladle, indispensable items for the job.

EQUIPMENT

Other accessories

The portable stove has another advantage which can prove extremely useful. **If you run out of alcohol, you can always use wood as a fuel.** Have you ever enjoyed a partridge on a spit, or rabbit perhaps ? If you have a grill available, I recommend that you take some venison or moose steaks with you. Certainly try a stuffed trout wrapped in aluminum. You will not be able to pass it up. And don't forget to toast marshmallows!

I always add some small pieces of wood to maintain the flame so long as I am awake. This allows me to warm up my hands, dry clothes, heat up soup, etc. The very glow of the fire adds to the tranquility of the camp. I often try to keep it going all night.

A partridge on a spit

Other accessories

LOADING THE SLED

The first and probably most important character-istic of a sled is without doubt its sturdiness. A sled is often used in demanding situations and this certainly is not the time to be presented with problems in its con-struction. The second important consideration is the manner in which it is packed. One must be prepared for long races, extended outings or expeditions, by maxi-mizing storage space. This requires some planning. There aren't dozens of solutions, but each piece of equipment or baggage should have its own specific place. Think of the order of activities and unforeseen possibilities relative to equipment. Then make a storage plan and implement it. All expert mushers know that meticulous planning is nearly as important as the aptitude of your dogs. Those participating in short 5 mile runs will need a light weight sled unencumbered with baggage. For those thinking of long treks or expeditions, your early planning will be well appreciated once you are well out on the trail.

To be sure, you will need to find space for a portable stove, maybe a naphtha lantern, a few dishes and cooking pots. If you will be sleeping "under the stars", a good sleeping bag and a small tent would be practical. Other equipment can be less obvious, but nevertheless useful. A cooler for me is essential, not only for keeping foodstuffs frozen, but also (if desired) for keeping things such as medications or batteries from freezing. Envision the worst scenarios and be prepared! Don't forget your snowshoes, your axe, a first aid kit and a few tools. In brief, if you have stowed absolutely everything for any and every event, your dogs will not be able to take off with this sled.

Other accessories

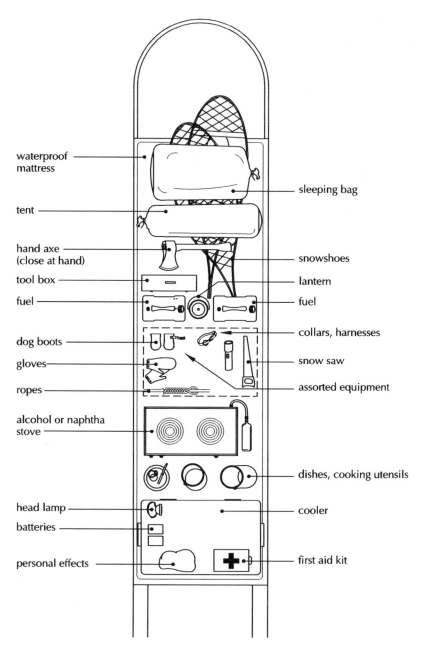

waterproof mattress

sleeping bag

tent

hand axe (close at hand)

snowshoes

tool box

lantern

fuel

fuel

collars, harnesses

dog boots

gloves

snow saw

ropes

assorted equipment

alcohol or naphtha stove

dishes, cooking utensils

head lamp

cooler

batteries

personal effects

first aid kit

Other accessories

PACKING THE SLED

A specially adapted wheather proof bag, covering the entire basket is almost a must, and can be indispensable if it rains, if the sled tips or to carry an injured dog. Put a waterproof mattress about 1 inch thick on the bottom of your sled bag.

Personal Objects

First aid kit, toilet paper, sunglasses, medications, spare clothing such as rainwear, felt inserts for boots, gloves, sleeping bag, tent, hand-warmers, compass, topographical maps, flashlight and batteries, a lighter, a knife, a pair of pliers, adhesive tape, a screwdriver kit, brass wire, food, nuts, chocolate, tin containers, money, credit cards, matches, etc...

For the Dogs

Two harnesses, a snubline, a towline section, stakeout line, two dog coats, two collars, dog boots, snaps, commercial dog food, meat, fish, feeding bowls, a shovel, garbage bags, cable lines and snow hooks.

Assorted Supplies

Plastic basket toboggan sled, snowshoes, an axe with a 24 inch long handle, a cooler, a snow saw, a soup ladle, a portable stove, stove fuel, a cooking pot, cooking utensils, a lighter and emergency flares.

Optional

Plastic shoes for the sled, an ice drill, fish hooks, monofilament, a firearm and an ice chopper.

Not to be Forgotten

Good humour, courtesy, patience...

Other accessories

GEE POLE

Altough you rarely see this tool in Québec, a gee pole may be invaluable if you have to carry a heavy load on a very bad trail. It is most probably the best way to travel with two people using the same dog team. I strongly suggest that you try it on a nice level trail to prepare yourself for any special situations. Any straight 9 to 10 foot dry pole which usually is easy to find should do the job. Install it to a comfortable height and solidly tie it to the side of the sled. Skis should be short for maneuverability, wide for good floatation and stability, and most important easy to put on and off your feet (like a skiboot quick release). Riding with a gee pole is almost like skijoring with a 10 dog team, but remember that if the driver at the back is not good with the brake, say your prayers, since you have no way of slowing down your team, except by tipping the sled on its side.

Of course, you have to put a small cable between the bungee and the gangline, or at least to put only one wheeler to make space for you. There is no excuse not to try it, with very little practice you will realy enjoy it. It is such a nice feeling to be with the dogs, in front of the sled.

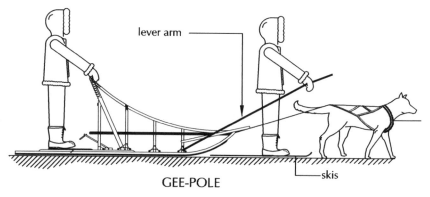

GEE-POLE

Other accessories

SKIJORING

If you have sled dogs, sooner or later you will be tempted to run them in front of you while you are on skis. Manufacturers of sled dog equipment have developed a wide, padded belt which is both secure and comfortable. At the front of this belt is a quick-release system that allows you to detach yourself quickly from your dogs in case of emergency. A regular gangline for leaders is used with a bungee to complete the system between you and your dogs. Europeans use cross country skis with a specially adapted harness. Personally, I always use my downhill skis and have found them to be more than adequate mainly for braking. Skijoring affords an excellent method for the training of lead dogs. Obviously one must have a certain degree of competence on skis. The dog chosen should be honest and have displayed reliability in other training as the braking capability of skis is limited. I have occasionally used skijoring as a method of training a young dog who has refused to pull in a team context.

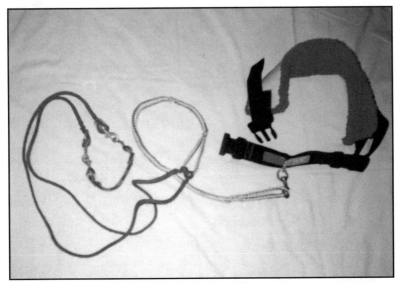

Padded skijoring belt and line system

EQUIPMENT

Other accessories

TRAIL DRAGS

Unless you are training on trails specifically prepared for sled dogs, you will probably be using trails being used by snowmobiles, all terrain vehicles or horses. The holes left in trails by horses' hooves, or tire ruts from ATVs create an injury risk for the feet of your dogs and make driving a sled very difficult. A solution to this problem is to build a trail drag. The trail drag may be flipped over onto its wheels to cross paved areas. Pulling an old wire fence section at the back of your sled will do about the same thing, and also help your dogs to develop their muscles.

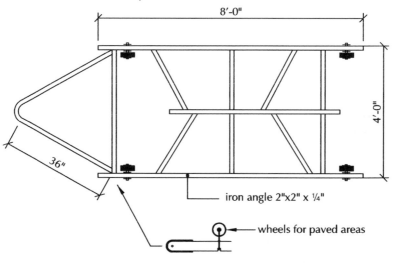

8'-0"

4'-0"

36"

iron angle 2"x2" x ¼"

wheels for paved areas

TRAIL DRAG

Musher wear

Can you imagine being cold not just for a few minutes, but for several hours? There is nothing worse. The solution should be simple, but it is not. It is rare that the temperature will vary more than 20° degrees Farenheit during the same outing (morning 0°F; noon -20°F to 20°F). The activity level during this time will also be variable. The musher will have periods of relative immobility riding the back of the sled and then other times be pushing the sled up steep inclines. Weather can vary from freezing rain to a white out snow storm to springtime sunshine. There are no magic solutions for clothing choice so, **think "multi-layers" and "efficiency".**

Before addressing the practical aspect of choosing clothing, I think that a quick review of the mechanisms of heat loss would be helpful. If your clothing does not allow an appropriate level of ventilation you will become too hot or too cold. Body heat must be dissipated at a rate equal to its production. Consequently, because body heat production levels vary as does the exterior temperature, you will have no choice but to choose clothing that can adapt to all these conditions.

HEAT PRODUCTION

Your body changes chemical energy from foods eaten (or stored fats) into heat by a series of complex mechanisms.

* These mechanisms keep your body temperature at about 98.6°F. The Inuit with their wealth of practical experience convinced me of the necessity of eating something at least every two hours. Gross energy values for mixed carbohydrates, fat and protein average 1867, 4267 and 2565 Kcal/pound. **Don't forget to eat**

cheese, nuts, butter and meats, etc., not only at meal time but also when you feel cold.

* Physical exercise creates enormous quantities of heat. This is why when you are very active you feel warm even if the ambient temperature has not changed. The real problem with heat dissipation is humidity. During intense exercise, **the body also releases humidity which can diminish the insulating qualities of your clothing.** If this humidity is not allowed to escape, you will feel cold when you reduce the activity level. In this event, it is important to dry your clothing as soon as possible. Happily, evaporation will help you here. Even in very cold temperatures, simply airing your clothing and sleeping bag will accomplish the task.

* **Heat produced by an organism is equalized throughout the body by the circulatory system**. Therefore, make sure that boots and mittens are large enough to allow for good blood circulation in the extremities. Pay attention too, to your ears which are particularly susceptible to freezing. It is important to note that injuries or stress reduce efficiency of blood flow. It is at these times that one will also feel cold. It is always preferable to be a little too warm!

* Alcohol gives the impression of feeling warmer. What in fact it does, is to dilate superficial blood vessels and therefore release heat on the skin surface. This may be the body heat that should not be lost, particularly in this environment, and may have negative effects even on internal organs. **Cafeine, contained in coffee, tea, chocolate, pepsi, coke, etc... reduces blood circulation in the extremities (fingers, ears and toes). Chicken or beef soups or bouillons are highly recommended.**

Musher wear

HEAT LOSS

The respiratory system plays an important role in both heat and water loss. Respiration and evaporation are forms of heat loss, mainly when sleeping outside. So drink plenty of fluids with your meals. The rest of heat loss depend on total skin surface, and therefore your clothing and sleeping bag will help in separating body surface from ambient air. The phenomena contributing to heat loss are :

Conduction

All materials conduct heat. Only a vacuum can give perfect insulation. In general, the more a material is dense, the more heat it will conduct. Air is an excellent insulator, a fact which is taken into account in the manufacturing of winter clothing. This is why tight clothing, where there is no place for air, is not as warm as loose clothing. Water, on the other hand, conducts heat very well. This is why humidity trapped in clothing will make you feel cold. Damp clothing will reduce considerably the efficiency of a coat or boots.

Radiation

Our body emits waves of heat as a function of its temperature. This is why a thin blanket of reflective material will keep you warm in bed. It simply reflects warmth (survival blanket) your body has given off back to you. In general light colors reflect radiation waves, and dark colors absorb them.

Ventilation

Your clothing must protect you against wind and drafts. In recent years fabrics have been developed which protect against wind as well as allowing for dissipation of humidity. Head coverings are very important because a large amount of body heat is dissipated through the head. A hood is almost a must in preserving heat by creating an air cushion around uncovered parts of the head.

Other Factors

Take into account the value of sunlight as a heat source. In competition, many mushers will run their dogs at night and sleep during the warmth of the day. The colder night temperatures are compensated for by the increased physical activity of the dogs and the driver. When bedding down to sleep, keep with you in your sleeping bag some of the clothes that you will wear when getting up. Cold weather is an excellent dryer (sublimation), mainly because humidity level of the air is almost nil.

UNDERWEAR

Choose underwear according to your activity level. Generally, they should be warm, comfortable and capable of absorbing moisture. Be sure to dry them thoroughly each day so they will keep their warmth qualities. Try them out a few times before extended trips to be sure you do not have allergies or irritations to the fabric. Personally, I use thermal underwear and a two piece polypropylene combination.

MITTENS - GLOVES

A musher is always faced with a dilemma mittens will keep his hands warm but they are difficult to work in; gloves are not efficient in keeping hands warm but one can work in them. Usually in milder weather, mushers will work in gloves or with their bare hands. When it is colder, gloves will be used for manipulating

Musher wear

equipment such as harnesses and snaps. Then a pair of mittens will be worn over the gloves.

Blood circulation is the regulator of global body temperature. This is particularly true for feet, hands and ears where heat loss is the greatest. To keep these warm, dress appropriately, and maintain good blood circulation with appropriate exercise. **Don't wait until hands and feet are cold to intervene with corrective measures. By then blood vessels in those areas will be highly restricted and the warming process will take much longer.** Sticky aluminum tape is an excellent insulator for hands or boots because it will reflect escaping heat back to the hands or feet.

Personally, I use light weight deer hide gloves inside a pair of mitts in colder weather. Then I can keep something on my hands when working with small articles such as snaps and when finished, put on the mitts. So my mitts don't get lost, I attach them to my coat with safety pins. Each of my sleds is equipped with a fur sleeve which has proven useful time and time again. What comfort to put cold hands in them and feel the warmth come back! They are also useful as a storage area for more fragile necessities such as sunglasses, a compass, and a whistle (for breaking up dog fights), etc. Indispensable...

SWEATERS

Given the enormous variations in temperature and activity levels, you need to be prepared to adjust the type of clothing you are wearing. A woolen sweater is designed to meet this need. Why not knit a sweater with the fur from your dogs? During moulting time, keep the wooly undercoat which is shed. Certain craft people will be able to convert this into a highly priced sweater. You will be awed by the final result. For more information, contact, MS THERESE GODETTE, R.R. #1, Apple Hill, Ontario, Canada, K0C 1B0, tel. 613-528-4630 or MS ESTHER CAVANAGH, 650 R.R. # 138, Huntingdon, Québec, Canada, J0S 1H0, tel. 450-264-6667.

COATS

Good coats vary in price between $150. and $1,000. The price generally is directly proportional to the quality. Each of us will buy according to what we need and what we can afford. Personally, I have opted for two piece suits which permit me to remove the heavy pants in warmer weather. I like loose clothing even if it reduces the level of agility. To my coat I add a fur ruff around the hood. Although it reduces my peripheral vision, the extra warmth around my face more than compensates for this minor disadvantage. I also add leather patches over the knees of my pants to reduce dampness from kneeling in the snow or while working with the dogs. In effect, your outer wear must protect you from wind and cold and must have some impermeability to moisture. Someone in the city can probably tolerate cold for a limited time, but a musher cannot spend hours shivering!

FUR

No matter what, one day your faithful companion will no longer open his eyes. I know that most of you will bury your friend. Sometimes, however, with the assistance of a taxidermist, you may wish to preserve the pelt for future memories. You will be surprised at the quality of northern breed dog pelts. Eight pelts are sufficient to make a coat with a hood. Fur coats are

Musher wear

very warm in cold northern climates and certainly more ecologically friendly than those manufactured in **Taiwan** from synthetic fibers.

BOOTS

Some people feel the cold more than others. Wear boots that are made for temperatures in which you are working. Besides being warm, boots must be waterproof and still allow running behind a sled or putting on a pair of snowshoes if necessary to break trail. I use **Sorel®** boots which have proven satisfactory up to - 50°F. For colder temperatures I use Bunny boots over my **Sorels'**. Again, it is important to remove and dry the inside felts almost every night. A spare insert is almost a must.

Ashley with bunny boots

All terrain vehicle

Mushers have developed a whole range of vehicles (gigs or rigs) more or less adapted to the conditions of the trails on which they train. Ideally, **the gig must be light, able to turn easily, possess brakes which lock in place and have a low centre of gravity.** Most mushers now use an All Terrain Vehicle (ATV), which, although very heavy, can respond to almost all situations. On trails which are not too rough, ten dogs are adequate, but if the trails are hilly, one usually uses the motor to assist the dogs. However, the dogs learn quickly to listen for the motor when the force required increases. This might lead to problems later, for when the dogs are hooked to a sled they may await the motor before exerting increased force. I discovered that golf carts are ideal, mainly because two people can sit comfortably, but you need many dogs even if the motor and battery have been removed.

When do you begin training? This depends entirely on you and what you expect of the dogs. For simple pleasure trips, a month of conditioning should be enough. For short races (less than 20 miles), two months are recommended. For long expeditions, a special training program, practically year round, must be planned. Cool autumn nights (Sept., Oct., Nov.) usually allow training of many miles each week. One must be careful, because the dogs don't protect themselves. Even if it is very warm, they try to run the same as though it were cold.

In temperatures too warm for training, I let some dogs run free together in a field or in a fenced-in area. This is good for the dogs' attitude. They get exercise and they learn to run alongside each other.

Buffy, Poppy, Blanche Neige, Blizzard, Polar, North Star, Zamouray, Trapper, Taku, Arctic and Geneviève

Black Snow, Poppy and Bernard

Mountain bike

During the summer, the dogs become bored, and probably you are also. A bicycle, as simple as possible, strong and used, is all that you need because using it in this manner, a new one will be like a rented one after only a few trips. It is very dangerous to ride with more than one person on a bicycle, mainly if the passenger is a child.

This is a practical way of reminding your lead dogs of their job and of keeping yourself in shape. Early morning hours often allow you to do some running with one or two dogs. It is essential that you make sure the gangline doesn't get wrapped up in the front wheel. I used a skijoring belt which gives me full control of the pulling cable at all time.

During the autumn and spring, this is truly great fun, but be sensible, don't hook up more than three dogs. A helmet, glasses, knee guards and very good boots are essential. A quick release to let the dogs go from you in emergency situations, will help to prevent injuries both to you and your dogs.

Regularly check your dogs' feet. Avoid at all costs paved or crushed stone roads. Walk the trail before you head out with your dogs. Make sure it is not too rough. Dogs have the unfortunate tendency to speed up going downhill, and your brakes will not be very effective. Sometimes your dogs will get a thorn or something similar in their pads. They are usually easy to take out. However, if your dog attacks a porcupine, see your veterinarian. Don't forget to take a small bag and a shovel to pick up after your dogs, particularly if you use bicycle paths.

Transport

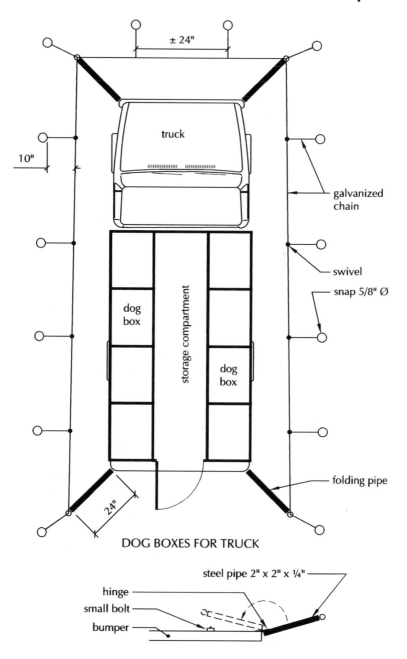

DOG BOXES FOR TRUCK

Transport

Even if your kennel is in the country, near trails, transporting your dogs and equipment is always a concern that you try to resolve in a variety of ways. If you own less than four dogs, and a vehicle that is at least adaptable, using commercial dog crates of galvanized steel wire or fiberglass, ought to be adequate. If your kennel is larger you must consider more efficient ways.

Many owners of small trucks anchor a chain inside their truck box. Onto this chain are attached secondary ones about 12 inches long. This system can handle up to a dozen dogs. For short trips, less than 15 miles, one can transport the team this way, but at a reduced speed depending on the outside temperature. However, this method is not too good for the dogs, especially during very cold weather.

Most mushers who own a small truck have a box fitted with compartments around 18 inches x 24 inches x 22 inches high. An opening with a protective grill allows the dogs both ventilation and a view of the countryside; this window is normally part of the door. Traditionally, straw in each compartment is used as bedding for the dogs' comfort. The center of this box serves as storage for equipment and dog food. In most cases the sled or sleds, are tied onto the top of the box. Various systems have been created by owners to tie the dogs around the truck. This setup has great advantages and ensures a relative comfort for the dogs. In fact, the dogs love their travelling kennel so much that they eat the doors, break the grills pushing their heads out the openings, etc. To prevent the dogs being stolen or simply the door opening on its own, there must be a locking device on each door.

Transport

Clearly, these solutions assume you own a truck, which isn't always so. The purchase of another vehicle, the insurance and maintenance costs are always rising. Also, just like some other mushers, I have decided to use an old skidoo trailer with similar arrangements. The additional space available compensates for the difficulties involved in hauling a trailer. The risk of the trailer being stolen must also be considered. A stop of ½ hour must be made every four hours, except for puppies, who must fulfill their needs more frequently.

Transport

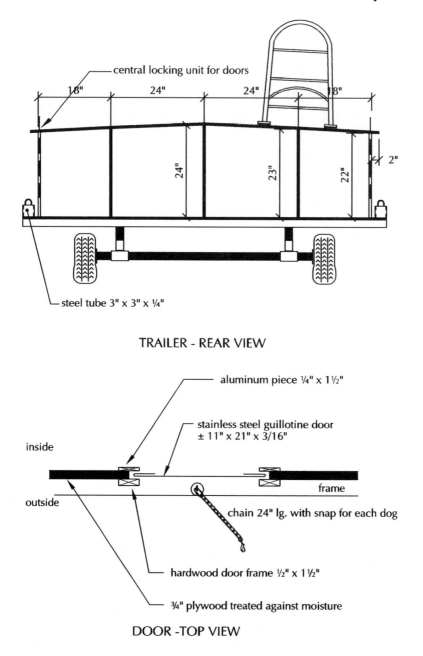

central locking unit for doors

18" 24" 24" 18"

24" 23" 22" 2"

steel tube 3" x 3" x ¼"

TRAILER - REAR VIEW

aluminum piece ¼" x 1½"

stainless steel guillotine door
± 11" x 21" x 3/16"

inside

frame

outside

chain 24" lg. with snap for each dog

hardwood door frame ½" x 1½"

¾" plywood treated against moisture

DOOR -TOP VIEW

Transport

Whatever the style of transport, it is important to plan a method of attaching your dogs around your vehicle. The best way to prevent damage to your vehicle is to have your dogs a good distance from it. Use outrigger bars in the front and back of the truck and attach a long chain to these. Small chains are easily attached to this main chain to which the dogs are snapped, far enough from each other to prevent them becoming entangled and from touching the vehicle.

Most of those who raise sled dogs also own snowmobiles or ATV's, and have a flat bed trailer to transport them. It is necessary to note that for training we often have to transport an ATV as well as our dogs.

I have benefitted from the fact that I have a skidoo trailer, 8'-0" x 8'-0" to adapt to my new needs. Also, I have built two removable sections, each having three compartments around 18 inches wide, 32 inches long and 22 inches high, allowing space for six dogs. This leaves a space around ± 4 feet wide in the centre of the trailer to transport an ATV, snowmobile or my golf cart. One word to describe this set up is that it is highly practical and as flexible as you wish, because these two sections can be removed when I no longer need them. In order to avoid using metal hinges, which rust. I have installed dropping doors and am satisfied with them. Protect the underside of your trailer with an anti-rust treatment.

I have also built another section, also removable, which fits between the two side sections and which adds four large compartments of ± 24 inches x 48 inches, each large enough for two dogs (it is warmer for the dogs). The removable sections do not need a bottom since the trailer has a wooden floor. It is then easy to

EQUIPMENT

Transport

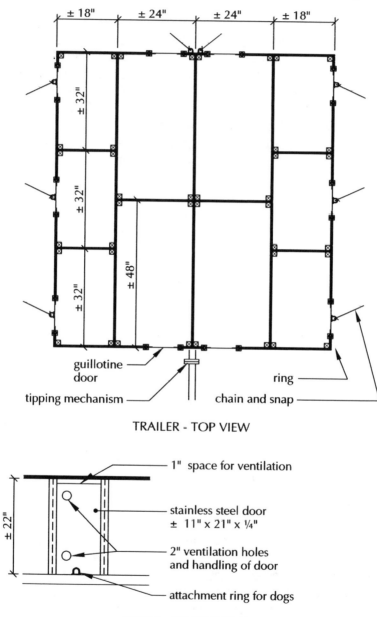

± 18" ± 24" ± 24" ± 18"

± 32"

± 32"

± 48"

± 32"

guillotine door

tipping mechanism

ring

chain and snap

TRAILER - TOP VIEW

1" space for ventilation

stainless steel door
± 11" x 21" x ¼"

2" ventilation holes
and handling of door

± 22"

attachment ring for dogs

DOOR - FRONT VIEW

Transport

carry two sleds on top of these sections, along with 14 dogs.

In short, **I think I have modified this design at least 3 times every month** for more than a year. I have finally developed a style of transport that I consider practical, particularly for short distances. I don't want to tell you how many doors and door frames my dogs ate before I decided to use stainless steel doors, 1/16 inch thick. Also, avoid an error I have had to take time to correct. The removable sections do not need a bottom since the trailer has a wooden floor. I used to put some old carpeting in each compartment. My dogs ate them and the carpets were always damp. **It took me many months to realize that straw is much better as bedding.** Don't forget to find a method of locking the doors. Your dogs, possibly, are smarter than you think.

The doors must be exactly the same dimensions to be interchangeable. The chains must be long enough to allow the dogs to touch but not to become entangled. All construction must be done with screws. Nails don't tolerate vibration and nailed boxes shift, making replacement difficult. A final piece of advice: try to put the same dog in the same compartment. One can let the dog loose, and he'll head directly to his place. The one disadvantage : You must travel slowly with such a light trailer, because it bounces on bumpy roads.

Enclosed trailer

Transport

If you plan to transport your dogs long distances, or in very low temperatures, the enclosed trailer represents great luxury. I personally have chosen an enclosed trailer, 7'-6" wide by 16'-0" long with a rear door and an access ramp. I have fitted it with 21 fixed compartments and 8 removable compartments around ± 33 inches wide by ± 21 inches deep by ± 22 inches high with the front open. A short chain 16 inches long keeps each dog from leaving the floor of each compartment. No more problems with doors gnawed by the dogs, rusted hardware, water and snow getting in. What a pleasure to see the dogs so comfortable. If they are unhappy, they don't look it. My sleds usually are tied to the top of my truck but can fit in the center of my trailer. I keep the top shelves of my trailer for baggage. I have installed mesh doors in 3 compartments to carry puppies.

I have seen this type of trailer in Alaska, however, I had not truly considered all the advantages. I had assured myself that this aids the spirit of the team. Now I have been able to check it out not only with the dogs but also with myself. When my friends are shivering outside, protected from the elements, I simply prepare the meal for my dogs and repair equipment in complete tranquility. In fact, I have definitely appreciated the roof during the cold rains of autumn and spring.

My mushing friends had some questions on this type of transport. One had predicted fights, damage, injuries, etc. My dogs certainly didn't hear that, for they always behave like angels.

If you wish to spoil your dogs, this should be considered. If you can afford to spoil yourself, this type of travelling kennel is a must.

Transport

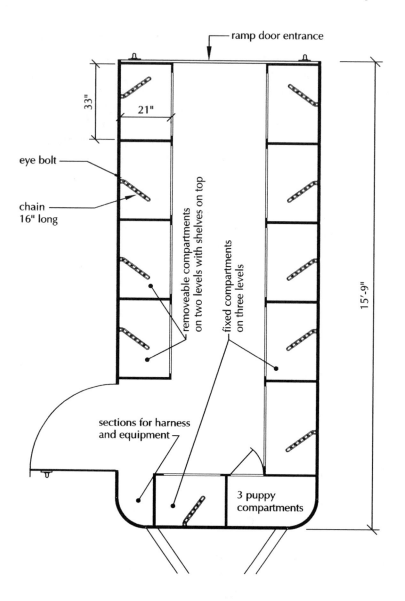

ramp door entrance

33"

21"

eye bolt

chain
16" long

removeable compartments
on two levels with shelves on top

fixed compartments
on three levels

15'-9"

sections for harness
and equipment

3 puppy
compartments

CLOSED TRAILER

Transport

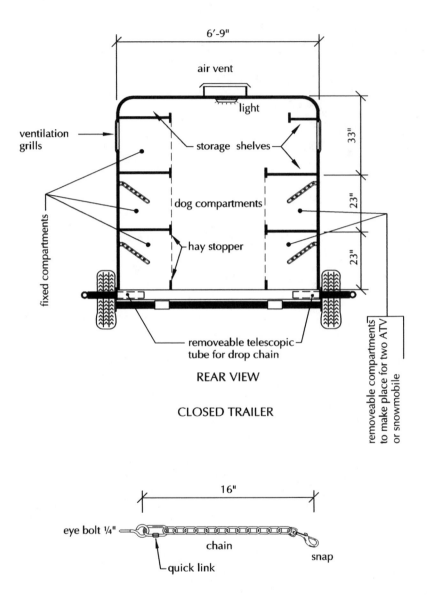

REAR VIEW

CLOSED TRAILER

DROP CHAIN

Transport

PASSENGERS

It is always very dangerous to carry people in the basket of a sled, because if you happen to loose control, it is very hard to say how this ride will end. A still passenger in the sled will always be cold, regardless of the amount of clothing worn, because of the absence of movement. This is especially true for a wounded person, so it is indispensable to supply auxilary heat such as hand warmers (charcoal, lighter fluid, or chemical powered).

For long distances, it is always better for the second person to drive a sled towed by the first sled. Certainly, the second sled must be equipped with a functional brake, and the driver must pay attention so as not to hit the first sled. In every way this is much more interesting and then, after one or two trips of this type, the passenger is usually ready to go alone with his own team.

Wasilia, Alaska, 1995

Bath time, Gérard, « Hanoré » and Donald

Ice fishing

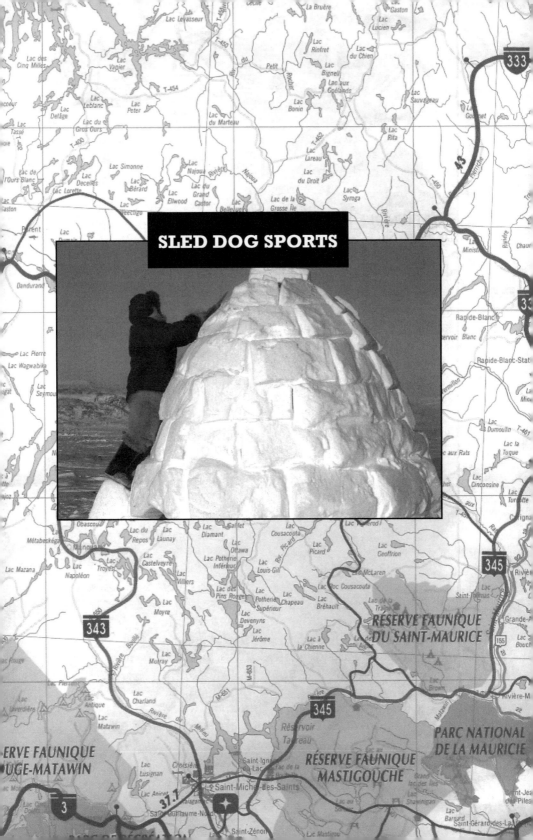

SLED DOG SPORTS

Training

One can't learn to swim by reading a book! Driving a dog sled is no different. You will have to learn by experience. Newcomers today have the advantage of certain basic guidelines.

You must feel comfortable on your sled. The distance between the runners will dictate in part the degree of stability you can expect. The handlebar should be high enough so that you can stand straight up on the sled. Any height less than this will result in a sore back if you spend extended time on the sled. Once en route, **don't hang onto the handle bar for dear life - relax a bit, and give your arms a rest**. Otherwise in an hour or so you will have aching arms. Be alert, relax and enjoy the scenery. When turning, unlike downhill skiing, you will put your weight on the runner of the side to which you are turning. Practice lifting one side of your sled when negotiating a slope. Learn how to manage turns, avoid obstacles on the trail and get under (or over) dead trees which may have fallen across the trail. You can use your braking system to help control your sled on icy surfaces. Driving a dog team requires constant alertness and good reflexes. The main line to which the dogs are attached must be kept tight, otherwise you will be dealing with dogs tangled in the secondary lines.

Begin with two or three dogs on relatively simple (and therefore easy) trails. Do not go out with more dogs than you can control in any given situation. Doing so can result in injuries to you and/or your dogs. Put some weight in your sled. Have a friend go with you; he will be able to help in cases of unforeseen circumstances. If you are going out alone, let one of your friends know your itinerary. **Visitors new to driving dogs should always be accompanied on their early**

Training

outings. If you recall earlier words of wisdom, it is not easy to drive a dog team and it is even more difficult if you do not understand or know the canine team members.

Most new dog mushers greatly underestimate the importance of training. No matter what sector of dog powered sports is your personal bias, **the dogs will need training to develop their muscles and endurance**. Any dog who spends the summer on a tether line in front of his kennel or even free in a small enclosed area will be far from being in working form. As all marathoners, hockey players or skiers, the canine athlete will also need an exercise program to develop those skills. The dog will also need the training to remind him of what his job is. Even if he learned his primary function the previous year, a little recall as to the job at hand will reduce the amount of playing in harness or arguing with a neighbour.

If you live in Alaska, you have eight months available for sledding. Part of this time can be used for the preliminary training and conditioning of the animals. If you live in Fermont in northern Québec, you will have a little less time available on snow. But if you live farther south, a major obstacle for you will be the very short period of time in which snow is available. I live in the south west corner of Québec, very near the American border. Winter is very short and snow conditions are fickle. Because of this, my initial training and conditioning period is relatively short. Like the majority of mushers in this situation, I too must begin my season on a wheeled vehicle. At any rate, I suggest that you review, in general, training protocols for sled dogs.

Training

0 - 12 Weeks

Puppies at this stage spend most of their time with their mother and play together. They should be confined in a small, secure and protected space at least until 2 weeks of age. At 4 weeks, they will require more space - at least enough that they can stretch their legs. By six weeks behavioural patterns of each will be evident. Some will be more aggressive, others will be calm, others will seem shy.

After six weeks, the puppies should be moved to their own larger pen. The pen should be at least 10 feet x 12 feet to allow for the puppies' increased activity. Mom will now spend less time with them, visiting once a day for one-half hour. You, too, must visit the puppies and spend time with them. Take each individual for a short walk. This will familiarize the puppy with being away from his litter mates. Ask family members as well as visitors to spend some time playing with the pups. The animal behavioural specialists, **Scott** and **Pfaffenberger** found through many studies that the brain of a 7 week old puppy already has its adult characteristics. This period from 5-12 weeks is the ideal time for encouraging desired behaviour.

3 to 4 Months

Begin to familiarize your puppies with wearing a collar. Remember to check the collar frequently so that it does not become too tight as the puppy grows. On your walks begin initiating them with basic sled dog commands, i.e. WHOA, GEE, HAW. Two weeks after their last vaccinations is the time to begin their introduction into the main kennel. Take them in your arms one by one, and introduce them to the adults. Watch carefully as there will be those adults who may not appreciate the possibility of being replaced! Continued

Training

contact with humans at this time is also important. Gradually, the puppies will have to be introduced to other noises such as music, firearms, vehicle traffic or snowmobile traffic. Once a week, put a harness on the puppy and have him drag a light load. Increase the weight of this load on a weekly basis. Also during this time the puppies are attached to a tethering system which allows them to move about in a large circle. When you are feeding, train the pups to allow the removal of their food bowl. If later a child happens to try to take food or a bone he will be less at risk for a dog bite. Encourage the pups to jump up to the roof of their house. This is good exercise. Have the pups become familiar with the mode of transportation they will have as adults.

4 to 6 Months

At four months, it is time to hitch these future champions. The procedures for accomplishing this task are as variable as the number of mushers. My preference is to hitch puppies in a team where the front four dogs are relatively quiet by nature, and have first completed their own run. The pup should run alone, close to the back of the team. Wait long enough before you leave to be sure that the pup is ready to go. Take all the time you need to assure that this first experience is a positive one. Let a friend drive your sled, and you stay in the vicinity of the youngster. This will give him the confidence to start well. Then move to the front of the team and let them start. Encourage the young one to go. Normally, only a few seconds of observation will tell you if the pup is ready to pull. If not, and if he puts on the brakes, stop the team and remove the pup. Repeat the experience again in a few days. After a few dozen feet, if all goes well, continue the outing for not more than one mile. Stop and praise the pup at frequent intervals to let him know that you are pleased with what he is doing. When the run is completed, remove his harness and, using a leash, take him back to the kennel. Repeat this experience two or three times a week if possible. The pup must consider this as "fun time".

Some pups will absolutely refuse to run and will vigorously resist even to the point of being dragged. Sometimes I will simply let these pups run loose behind the team. I have also succeeded with some pups like this by running them beside their mother. Those for whom this is unsuccessful, are returned to the kennel and do not run again for a month.

7 -12 Months
Run the youngsters as frequently as possible, gradually increasing the distance up to three miles. Pups still refusing to work in harness or to run with the team are carried in the sled to about one mile from the kennel. At this point, the pup's ride is over. The team leaves with the handler staying with the pup. He slips on a pair of skis and attachs himself to the pup's harness. The pup will want to return to the kennel and so gradually will learn to pull. Normally, this is a very efficient training technique. After several such experiences, I will add another dog, a quiet one or his mother. After three or four of these outings, the youngster most often will be ready to take his place in the team.

Young dogs are particularly high-spirited. Their desire to run is remarkable, especially compared to older dogs, but their endurance is less than that of the adults. My outings for dogs less than 12 months never exceed 15 miles. With pups you will not have to run them as frequently as adults to maintain their training

Training

unlike the adults, they will spend their off days running and playing in their kennel space. Check their collars and harnesses frequently for sizing. Remember the pups are growing! The neckline should be at right angles to the main line. The end of the harness should fall in the region of the base of the dog's tail.

Take advantage of the pup's willingness to learn. When introducing new experiences, organize the activity in a fashion that ensures the pup's success in doing what you wish. Prevent brutal shocks. Don't ask them, as a first experience, to cross a highway during rush hour. Begin first by having them cross a short stretch of pavement or a concrete sidewalk. Gradually increase the distance of this experience until the pups don't even notice the difference in their footing. Try to avoid slippery surfaces - this nearly always creates a negative reaction. Present these types of surfaces in small doses and give the pups time to learn how to negotiate this type of footing.

At the end of their first year, the young dogs should be comfortable mentally and physically to cross a bridge, go across small creeks, cross a frozen lake, go through a tunnel, run on a railway right of way, cross a shallow pool of water, and work in deep snow.

Make sure that your pups learn their names, even if their names are called by a stranger or among the presence of other dogs. Useful, as well, is to have them learn the main commands that they will need to know. Don't dream ! I would be surprised if they stopped for more than 30 seconds in response to the command 'WHOA'!

Training

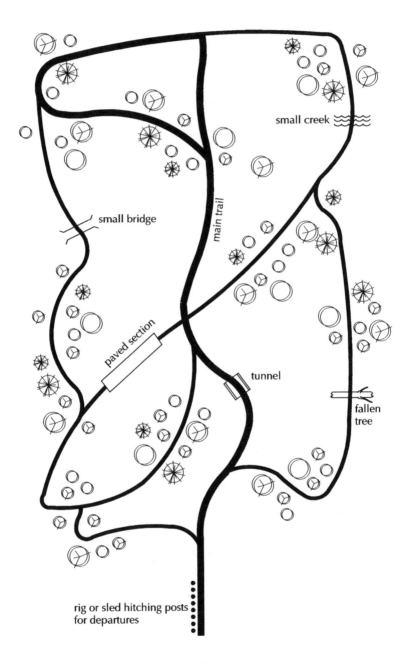

small creek

main trail

small bridge

paved section

tunnel

fallen tree

rig or sled hitching posts for departures

Training

12 to 24 Months

The pups are now adolescents with the associated mood swings. They are very active. They begin to assert their independence. The behaviour associated with sledding of the past several months will suddenly be forgotten. They seem to be saying: 'We want to play or maybe even to fight - we want to do our own thing!' Even you will be asking yourself 'What happened?'

This is still the time to try the pups in various positions in the team. Does the young dog prefer to run on the left or on the right? Is he better in wheel position or at swing? Does he show aptitude as a leader? At the same time you can verify the ability of older dogs to adjust to different team positions. Use this time to try the pups (one at a time) with an experienced leader, where they can begin associating turn commands with turning. At the end of this time you will have decisions to make. Personally, at the end of each run, I record information about each team member; the distance of the run, each dog's position in the team and his behaviour.

If you plan to do long distance running, don't forget to occasionally change the dog's position in the team. The two positions that are the most stressful are that of wheel and of lead. Others in the middle of the team will also appreciate being moved around if only to break the monotony. Most dogs will work well in nearly every position except as leaders. Obviously, you will also find that some dogs will dislike others; females are famous for this! Don't forget that you are dealing with the evolution of pack hierarchy, not dissimilar in characteristics to group activities in humans.

Training

If you discover a young dog with a particular aptitude for the lead position, reserve extra time for his development.   Concentrate on developing a good collaboration with him. The rest will follow in an appropriate time frame. For now, do not force this pup, do not apply formal training; rather capitalize only on his willingness to stay up front.   This dog must want to please you. But be careful to not be too familiar with him or you will have a dog who would rather be right at your side instead of running ahead into another new adventure. He must accept you as the leader of the pack and above all, trust you implicitly.   Resist the temptation to run this dog as a primary leader before the age of two years. An experienced leader beside the pup will provide a positive learning experience. Not doing so can result in problems that will be very difficult to correct. Pups with their inquisitive nature will be quick to try to follow freshly scented wildlife trails, or to stop to sniff a tree or simply to play at the base of a small shrub.

You will note that your pups do not develop at the same rhythm, or in the same fashion even if they are litter mates. You can expect the worst to happen at

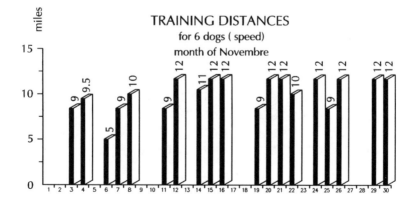

TRAINING DISTANCES
for 6 dogs (speed)
month of Novembre

Training

some time. I have seen dogs nearly two years old suddenly refuse to run for no apparent reason; dogs which I had to pull from the team for several weeks. This is one of the reasons that **I always have a dog bag on my sled**. Normally at the end of the second year the dogs understand what you expect of them. Eliminating dogs from your team now will most likely be due to reasons of injury or perhaps aggressive behaviour.

If you have a large enclosed compound, it is a good idea to give team members a short time to run loose together prior to leaving to let the pack reestablish its hierarchy. Other essential experiences include expeditions of several days. Team stability is essential in long expeditions. The experience of running many hours a day and sleeping together will reinforce their team spirit. In long distance expedition, after the dogs have attained their normal gait, try not to disturb them by talking, whistling, etc... They will also learn to sleep under the stars on a simple bed of spruce boughs.

24 Months and up.

Depending upon the activity that you plan to do, the frequency and distance of your outings will vary. Unfortunately, training is not simply getting out to run a few miles. Behaviour is also extremely important. Looking at directional training, there are as many tricks as mushers to have a team turn right or left. Personally I use an experienced dog to teach the new one. During the night, I use a head lamp to light up the new trail choice at the same time as a verbal command given. This works very well. I also will take the team to a trail with many intersections either 'Y's' or 'T's'. These multiple and frequent choices will help in learning 'GEE' and 'HAW'.

Training

Within a few weeks, the leaders will turn on command with few problems. If they make a mistake, all I do is say 'NO, NO, NO', braking, and repeating the correct turn command this will usually make them take the righ direction.

It is more difficult to teach trail reversal with the commands 'COME GEE' or 'COME HAW'. At the beginning of the winter, I put small loops (becoming smaller and smaller) near the end of my main trail to the right and to the left. This is normally enough to teach these commands. Teach this command when the team is less excitable and thereby less interested in any chicanery. Make sure the dogs learn to turn in a systematic fashion and not always at the same place.

To have the dogs speed up, I use the word "HOME". During my outings, I stop one final time just before arriving home. In early training this will be just a few hundred feet from the truck. The dogs see the truck and really want to finish.

Training

Then I say 'HOME' and we leave. They leave with great vigor and head for the truck at their maximum speed. The distance between this last stop and the finish is gradually increased as training progresses. By this time the dogs understand the command 'HOME'. Another useful command is 'SLOWLY'. Use the word at the same time as applying the brakes. Before long the dogs will slow their pace.

When overtaking another team, the training techniques follow the same principles. Working with a friend and a second team, stopped on the return trip a few meters from the truck, I will bring my team not far behind the other team and stop. When we leave with the command 'HOME', the dogs are far more interested in getting back to the truck than paying attention to the dogs stopped on the trail. Gradually the stopped team will be farther and farther from the truck. Later, working with a vehicle or snowmobile, the same training will apply.

Once the dogs are comfortable with overtaking another team, we begin the training for head-on passing. At the beginning I use wider trails and surveillance. If you already have two well trained leaders who will keep the team strung out, the pass should go well.

No matter what types of dogs you have, at some point you will be called upon to deal with fighting amongst them or with an other team. Sometimes, the best way to handle a fight is not to intervene until the fighters are exhausted. Just try to keep the other dogs away. Whistling to stop a fight, or to indicate your presence to another team can be very effective.

Training

This is not an unusual (albeit undesirable) happening. The majority of my dogs consider that the territory around their dog house is their private turf. So if a loose dog arrives to check out this territory, he may well be attacked by the other. When you are moving dogs around in the kennel, try not to directly cross too many "private territories". A male which has spent a few days with a female in season stands a good chance of being attacked by other males because of the odour he gives off. A new dog, a hurt dog or an old male can often be attacked by the rest of the pack. A female in season can provoke awesome fights. This same female will show her teeth to males who are too aggressive in their romantic pursuit. Do not feed dogs while they are loose. Rarely are there problems between dogs of different teams even when meeting and passing.

Most fights occur between members of the same team. Using double leaders reduces the incidence of fights as the main line is kept tighter. If one of the two makes an error, the other leader is there to assume the role of 'lining out the team'. Within a team, one will see on occasion a dog that keeps trying to turn back with the intent of attacking the dog behind him. Simple solution: switch their order in the team, or run them together where they will be forced to settle their differences.

During the training time a behavioural profile of each of your dogs will become evident. Some prefer to run on the right hand side of the main line, others on the left. Some will run with greater enthusiasm farther back in the team; others will be closer to the leaders. Then there will be those multi-talented animals that will do their job well in almost any position. Know your dogs well so that you can make appropriate position changes in long expeditions to help break the monotony. During

Training

training I like to leave an empty place available in the team set up. This allows changing dogs without having to hold onto two at the same time. Another advantage is providing a space for a dog that wishes to run alone.

I also make the leader tug lines longer and install a bungee section in them. This reduces the jerking motion on the leaders and allows them to maintain a steadier pull on the main line. It is not easy. Don't forget to carry extra collars, harnesses, gangline sections, snaps, etc. to deal with any eventuality.

One of my friends detaches the tuglines from the dogs when he is stopping for a small break. The dogs remain attached by the neckline only and can move around a bit in a non-working position. This autonomy helps to reduce the stress of a long working day.

If you wish to train on river surfaces or frozen lakes, be careful! Four inches of ice is enough to support even a heavily loaded sled. However, short of being on a lake without currents and eddies, it is very difficult to evaluate the variations in ice thickness. On river ice, water currents can reduce ice thickness without a visible sign. Similarly, decomposition of organic matter in marshes reduces the ice to practically nothing. Snow acts as an insulation over ice, and if you venture out in this context you risk having serious problems. It is absolutely false to believe that your dogs will recognize the danger of thin ice. **A golden rule : never sled with your dogs on frozen ice surfaces that you do not know extremely well.**

For fall and spring you can always use a wheeled vehicle for training. We hitch our leaders to regular trail bicycles. They love it, and to improve collaboration,

257

there is nothing like it. However, during the summer or when temperatures are greater than 50°F, you are better not to run. Use this time to educate your dogs.

Take more timid animals for walks in crowded, busy areas. With one dog, and a leash in hand, it won't take long until the animal understands the word WHOA. Work with young leaders in the same fashion; teach them GEE and HAW. If some avoid water on the trail, take them swimming with you. Sandy beaches are ideal places as dogs seem to enjoy romping in water that is not too deep. Here they can be initiated slowly to deeper water until they realize that they can swim. Communication between you and your dog in this context is almost easy. In effect they are receiving private lessons. The dog is not bothered by other dogs, and you are able to focus your attention on one animal instead of several. You will be astonished at the results. Limit these water lessons to not more than 15 minutes per day. The dog should not consider this exercise as a chore, but rather as a game. I would also recommend a limit of 2 or 3 days a week for these sessions. Wouldn't it be marvelous if you could go out sledding without concern next year. I would not recommend dog walkers as an exercising tool. The risk of accidents is too high (i.e. dog who refuses to follow the circuit could be choked to death).

I strongly recommend that health and training records be kept for each dog. This will come as an invaluable tool for the musher to make the right decision. Different computerized management programs are available (e.q. TOP DOG, Randy Carris, of Chaos Management, Cedar Rapids, Iowa).

HEALTH RECORD

NAME: *Blizzard*   WHELPED: 07-12-92   BREED: *husky*

FATHER: *Gizmo* (U.S.A)   LINE : *Anadyr*

MOTHER: *Thunder*   LINE : *Kimlan*

CANADIAN KENNEL CLUB NUMBER ~~AY2~~ AY218176   # CHIP : #221A604C38

SEX : M   COLOUR : *grey*   EYES : *blue*

ILLNESSES - TREATMENTS

12-06-98	*vaccination rabies etc ...*
18-06-98	*Benzelmin deworming*
8,9,10-12-98	*diarrhea— Neo—atropec*

INJURIES

12-12-97	*cut on right front foot*
5-01-98	*bite on nose*

SPECIAL NOTES

—needs boots on sticky snow
—fights with Anouk and ~~Mishka~~ Artic
  —stops frequently to urinate

TRAINING RECORD

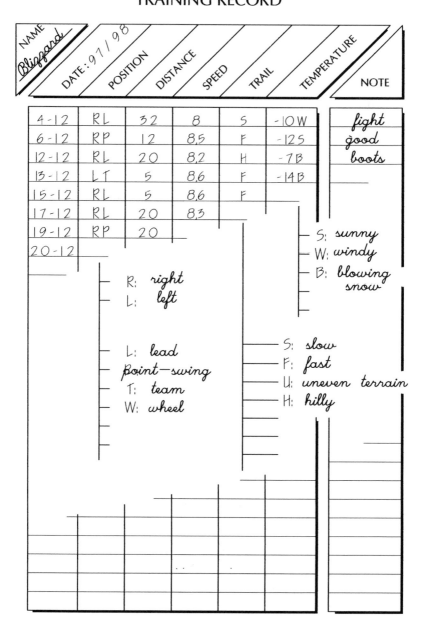

NAME Blizzard / DATE: 9 7 / 9 8	POSITION	DISTANCE	SPEED	TRAIL	TEMPERATURE	NOTE
4-12	RL	32	8	S	-10 W	fight
6-12	RP	12	8,5	F	-12 S	good
12-12	RL	20	8,2	H	-7 B	boots
13-12	LT	5	8,6	F	-14 B	
15-12	RL	5	8,6	F		
17-12	RL	20	8,3			
19-12	RP	20				
20-12						

R: right
L: left

L: lead
point—swing
T: team
W: wheel

S: slow
F: fast
U: uneven terrain
H: hilly

S: sunny
W: windy
B: blowing snow

Enjoying your dog team

In face of the growing demand for facilities supporting dog powered sports, many sectors of government, non-profit associations and outdoor activity centers are developing trails for sledding with dogs. Most of these organizations maintain trails from 10 to 30 miles, thus providing an area for mushers to train their dogs. The added advantage for mushers is the passing experience this system allows. Mushers can also observe other training methods and perhaps improve their own approach. Even if one has to transport his teams to these areas, the value in experience for both dogs and mushers is invaluable.

An excellent example of one such place is **"Le Centre de Plein Air les Forestiers"** situated in Saint-Lazare, Québec. Outdoor enthusiasts here have formed an association which manages the maintenance of trail systems dedicated to sled dogs and skijoring as well as cross country skiing. Several outfitters in Québec have realized the market potential of these outdoor activities. They offer, for example, holiday weekends, including maintained trails and hotel accommodations. Outings and competitions are also organized. Chalet accommodations used by fishermen and hunters in other seasons are usually very comfortable. Most have a wood stove, beds with mattresses only, as well as some utensils for cooking and serving meals. Some outfitters will even have a cafeteria.

Coopérative de solidarité de randonnée de chiens attelés du centre du Québec (1-819-385-4088). Many mushers from Québec province have gotten together recently to form a cooperative. Their main goals are :
> 1 - To negotiate passageway rights for sled dogs trails.

Enjoying your dog team

2 - To set up and maintain new sled dog trails.
3 - To implement a large new kennel for member's use.
4 - To negotiate with governments, cities, insurances, etc.
5 - To handle public relations (publicity, demonstrations, information, etc,).

This may be the ideal solution for sled dog owners who cannot provide all dog necessities.

Likewise, certain parks in both Canada and the United States have followed this lead and have developed trail systems for sled dogs. **La Réserve Faunique du St-Maurice** is a typical example. They maintain four primary trails varying in lengths from 10 miles to 40 miles (total 200 miles). Thirteen cabins equipped with wood stoves, beds and mattresses, table and chairs, etc. allow about 100 mushers to spend the night in the park. One can also participate in winter camping. These destinations are becoming more and more popular so phone to make reservations (1-819-646-5680). Even if these parks supply semi-sophisticated accommodations, the trail length does demand that the musher have some degree of experience. He must be able to cope on his own. The temperature can vary and you are not protected from problems that could result in spending the night outside. You must carry your own food, outdoor cooker, feeding utensils, as well as articles necessary for comfort and security (such as a compass, GPS). Above all, don't forget a good axe, a dog bag, and a shovel to clean up after your dogs. The rates are very reasonable. Normally on these trails one will meet mushing outfitters who offer outdoor vacation packages to those who wish to have this experience.

Enjoying your dog team

For those who do not have the dogs and equipment to do this, but would like to have the experience, there exist many businesses offering sled dog outings ranging from a few hours to one or two weeks in the Québec tundra (e.g. **L'Univers du chien de traîneau**). Most outfitters will even allow you to drive one of the teams. Obviously these dogs shine more because of their sociability than their speed! However, you will really appreciate these outings. It is an unforgettable experience for child and adult alike. For more information you can contact :

LA FÉDÉRATION QUÉBÉCOISE
DES SPORTS DE CHIENS ATTELÉS
Tel : 1-450-621-8558
Email : jylaporte@videotron.com

OR

L'UNIVERS DU CHIEN
DE TRAÎNEAU
Toll free : 1-888-880-2029
Fax : 1-450-373-9991
Email : apilonjr@rocler.qc.ca

In Québec many sled dog events are organized by both individuals and clubs without worrying about competition. In my opinion this is the best way to become initiated to our great outdoors. It is difficult, if not impossible, to organize a trek of several days into the wilds of Canada on your own. It demands far too much organization, not to mention questions of security. What a pleasure to travel near the end of March in a group and to camp at the edge of a small hidden creek. Imagine the scene at the end of the day, when everyones' teams are all settled around the camp fire.

Enjoying your dog team

Enchanting is not strong enough to describe the feeling. Don't, above all, bring a radio, a satellite television or a cellular phone. Each year, I arrange to work with a different group and in this fashion I discover another area of the country.

Personally, I believe that these types of activities are in a growth phase. There are many mushers who know that they have neither the time nor the money to consider professional racing. There are also persons who simply wish to get out to enjoy a more natural environment with friends or family without thinking of competing or winning prizes. If you have a team that you know is not competitive, don't be stubborn, you might just as well enjoy the activity.

At least once, I suggest that you take a tent and a small trapper's stove and spend a night camping along a trail with your dogs. Consider sleeping in your sled bag in case of emergency. If you have some time on your hands, you may wish to camp in the same area for several days. A small snow hut will make for more comfortable living.

During my hunting trips with the Inuit in Alaska, Yukon and the Canadian Northwest Territories, I had the experience of constructing and using an igloo for shelter. It is a lot easier than one would think and surprisingly comfortable. With outside temperatures at -50°F, I found that inside temperatures varied from +20°F at the floor to 40°F at shoulder levels, and this only from the body heat of the occupants.

An igloo with a diameter of 10'-0" will normally accommodate two people. Larger igloos are more difficult to build, not as warm and also less practical if

Enjoying your dog team

there are more than two people moving around. Normally people sit on a waterproof mattress covered with a sleeping bag at the entrance to the igloo. Nearby will be the stove, the lantern, utensils and personal effects. To sleep, one just has to stretch out towards the back of the igloo. An "L" shaped corridor is used to limit the entry of cold air and can also be used to keep a hurt dog. Two experienced people can construct an igloo in less than two hours. Those without experience will need twice as much time.

On the banks of lakes or rivers, find an area where the snowdrifts (at least six feet deep) have accumulated. Begin by packing the snow of the chosen area with your snowshoes. Wait about one-half hour to be sure that the crystalized snow has hardened. Define the perimeter of the igloo as well as the access corridor, taking into account the direction of prevailing winds. Then begin with your snow saw to empty the area that will be the entrance to the igloo. This area will be cleared just to the depth of the floor of the corridor.

Cutting snow blocks
Gjoa Haven, N.W.T., 1992

Enjoying your dog team

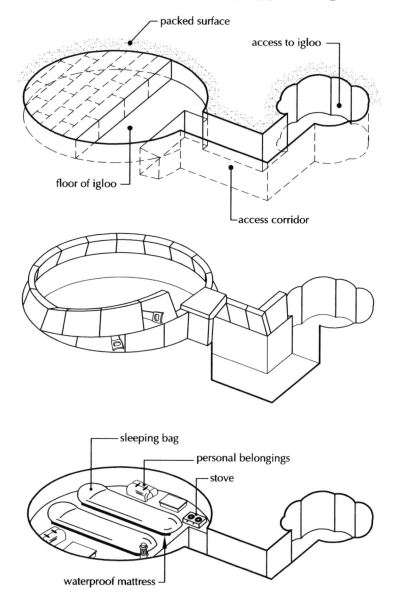

PLAN OF AN IGLOO

Enjoying your dog team

Open up the corridor by cutting blocks of snow (24 inches long by 18 inches high by 6 inches thick) from the area. Arrange these blocks on either side of the corridor. To cut the blocks, use a regular large toothed saw. Continue the work until you have cleared an area of approximately 18 inches wide at the interior of the igloo, for your feet. Then make the floor of the shelter about 18 inches higher (this area is for sitting or sleeping). Actual construction of the igloo is really very simple. The snow blocks are placed in a spiral fashion around the perimeter of the igloo with a slight cant towards the middle. Adjustments are made with the saw in a back and forth motion until each block settles in its proper position. Put the roof where the corridor meets the igloo first so that blocks creating the igloo walls will

Enjoying your dog team

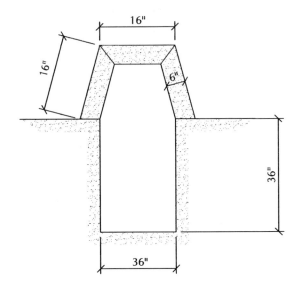

16"

16"

6"

36"

36"

ACCESS CORRIDOR

SNOW HUT

Enjoying your dog team

go over the top of it. Once the last block is in place to complete the igloo, create about a 4 inch opening in the ceiling for ventilation, especially if you are using a fuel stove. Now create an arch over the corridor (± 24 inches). Tap the exterior of the igloo with your shovel to ensure that all blocks are securely in place. Leave a candle burning day and night to keep the humidity down, and even to keep your coffee warm. You now have a second residence for the rest of the winter.

An even easier shelter is a snow hut. Choose an area with lots of snow and pack the snow down with your snowshoes where the hut will be. Using your shovel, add an additional 12 inch layer of snow to the area and then pack that down. Keep adding layers of 12 inches of snow until the snow pile is the height you wish (at least 10 feet). Then all you have to do is scoop out the interior of the snow pile being careful to leave thick enough walls & roof (at least 12 inches). Adding an "L" shaped corridor is almost a must. Don't forget a ventilation hole in the ceiling to allow the humidity to escape. This is very much like a beaver lodge.

In emergency situations, creating a small tunnel in the snow does not take very long. If the temperature is very bad, your dogs could benefit from this shelter too. To try a snow hut is to find a new way of living. I have a trap line in the La Vérendrye park. I leave you to imagine my sled dog team winding its way along narrow trails, crossing from one lake to another, stopping from time to time while I pick up a rabbit, a beaver or a fox. I won't even attempt to describe my trapping camp at the end of the day when I am preparing food for my huskies.

Is is a million miles away from the virtual world that the 20th Century has imposed upon us.

1994 INTERNATIONAL SLEDOD RACE ALPIROD®

YUKON QUEST Trading Company

Official YUKON QUEST "1996" Designs
Available September 1st, 1995
● T-shirts ● Sweatshirts ● Caps
● Patches ● Buttons ● Pins
And Much More

MAIL ORDERS ACCEPTED

558 2nd Avenue · Fairbanks, Alaska 99701 · (907)451-8985

TROPHEE JACK LONDON

PERCY DeWOLFE MEMORIAL MAIL RACE

Carried by Dog Team

SERRE CHEVALIER

INTERNATIONAL ROCKY MOUNTAIN STAGE STOP

LA "MASTIGOUCHE"

John **BEARGREASE**

Sled Dog Marathon

· SLED · DOG · RACE ·

LABRADOR 400

ALBERTA INTERNATIONAL SLED DOG CLASSIC CANMORE

CAN-AM CROWN

SLED DOG RACE
FORT KENT, MAINE

Défi du Lac-St-Jean inc.

Ste-Hedwidge, Québec
2 CLASSES

RENDEZ-VOUS GATINEAU

Races

Actually, I know (like all mushers) that I have the best sled dogs around and to compare them to others would be an insult. However, even if one has dogs only for pleasure, invariably they end up taking them either to competitions or to public demonstrations.

Most carnivals or outdoor activity centers are now organizing activities relating to sled dogs. Most often one will see competitions. There are some advantages in participating in these competitions.

With the increasing in the number of dog teams, competitions are popping up all over Québec and Canada. Each week-end we are able to choose from a number of available competitions. These races vary from 5 miles to hundreds of miles with teams of two to twelve dogs. More serious competitions here in Québec are sanctioned by the **"Fédération Québécoise des Sports de Chiens Attelés"**. Elsewhere in North America the sanctioning body is the **International Sled Dog Racing Association**.

If you attend these events as a spectator, please go without your dogs. A pet dog, even on a leash, can create problems of distraction for the canine athletes and could even result in fights or injuries. Before you decide to register your dogs in a demonstration or a race, make absolutely certain that your dogs are well trained and under your control. There is no place in demonstrations or in races for uncontrolled dogs. In larger races, some mushers will carry a whip and in some races even a firearm to be able to defend their team against stray dogs or even wild animals (wolves, moose, bears, etc...).

SLED DOG SPORTS

Races

At the international level. The major races are organized following the rules of the International Sled Dog Racing Association Inc..

1 - All races must have a qualified veterinarian present. This person will assure that all animals are in good health and have been vaccinated.

2 - Maltreatment of the dogs is not tolerated. Each sled must be equipped with a dog bag in which injured animals must be carried. In distance races this will be to the next official check point; in sprint races this will be to the end of that day of racing.

3 - The Chief Judge of the competition has the exclusive privilege of rule interpretation and will make decisions concerning such things as changing trail routes to ensure the safety of the dogs, applying penalties for rule infractions, etc.

4 - Drugs influencing the animal's behaviour, masking injuries, suppressing the symptoms of illnesses are not allowed. Random urine & blood testing can be done.

5 - A musher can help another driver in difficulty; this musher can then go on to finish the race. When a team catches up to another competitor he can ask for 'TRAIL'.

6 - In distance racing the following equipment must be carried in the sled : a sleeping bag, an axe, a pair of snowshoes, a knife, a head lamp, a stove, dog boots, etc.

7 - At the finish line, the nose of the lead dog of a team, with the musher controling his sled, determines the official time of the team.

Races

<u>MAJOR RACES</u>
Patagonia - Great Andes Race
5 x 60 miles, Argentina
Tel/Fax : 54-17712807

Norwegian Long-distance Championship
8 - dogs, 180 miles; open, 300 miles
Roros, Norway, Fax : 47-1492076454

International Sled Dog Race of Schmallenberg
Schmallenberg, Germany
Tel/fax : 63-2458592

British Cup Sled Dog Race
Glenisla, Scotland
UK 44-1992-629362

International Sled Dog Race of Laengenfeld
Laengenfeld, Austria
Tel/Fax : 63-2458692

Algoma Sled Dog Club Winter Warmup 100
10-dogs; 100 miles, Bruce Mines, Ontario
Tel : 705-736-2332 or 705-785-1002

Gold Rush Trail Sled Dog Race
Quesnel-Wells, British Columbia
Tel : 604-249-5710

The Marmora Cup
150 miles, Marmora, Ontario
Tel : 800-727-2962

Husqvarna Challenge
150 miles, Hudson's Bay, Saskatchewan
Tel : 306-865-3344 or 306-865-4135

North Star

SLED DOG SPORTS

Wildcat Mushers Marathon
500 miles, Hudson's Bay, Saskatchewan
Tel : 306-865-3344 or 306-865-4135

Défit du Lac St-Jean
200 miles, Sainte-Hedwidge, Québec
Tel : 418-275-1868

Le week-end blanc
4,6,8, ill., Saint-Donat, Québec
Tel : 819-424-2833

Labrador 400
400 miles, 100 miles, Labrador City, Terre-Neuve
Tel : 709-944-7155

Percy De Wolfe Memorial Mail Race
210 miles, Dawson City, Yukon
Tel : 403-993-6851

Alberta International Sled Dog Classic
4,6,8,10-dogs, Canmore, Alberta
Tel : 403-678-2692

Voyageur International Sled Dog Classic
4,6,10-dogs, Winnipeg, Manitoba
Tel : 204-237-7692 or 204-253-1401

Bell Atlantic Westline Classic
6,10-dogs, Westline, Pensylvania
Tel : 814-723-7546 or 814-778-5103

John Beargrease Sled Dog Race
10, 16-dogs, Duluth, Minnesota
Tel : 218-722-7631

Races

UP 200 Sled Dog Championship & Midnight Run
6, 10-dogs, Marquette, Michigan
Tel : 906-428-9307

Race to the Sky
300 - 500 miles, Helena, Montana
Tel : 406-442-2335 or 406-442-4008

Two Rivers Mushers Assoc.
200 miles, Two Rivers, Alaska
Tel : 907-488-3114 or 907-488-4135

Copper Basin 300
300 miles, Glenallen, Alaska
Tel : 907-822-3663

Klondike 300, Aurora International
300 miles, Big Lake, Alaska
Tel : 907-892-6261

Kuskokwim 300
300 miles, Bethel, Alaska
Tel : 907-543-3300

Yukon Quest International Sled Dog Race
1000 miles, Fairbanks, Alaska
Tel : 907-452-7954

Iditarod Trail Sled Dog Race
1049 miles, Anchorage, Alaska
Tel : 907-376-5155

Arctic

Races

THE IDITAROD

The **IDITAROD** is without doubt the most media exposed of all races. It crosses Alaska from Anchorage to Nome, a distance of about 1000 miles. It starts on the first Saturday of March in Anchorage with each team allowed a maximum of 16 dogs. Around 10 days later, having crossed Alaska, the first teams begin to arrive at Nome on the West Coast of Alaska, some hundred miles from Russia.

About 26 check points are set up along this historic trail to resupply the teams as well as to provide medical care. Fifteen hundred volunteers work throughout the year to organize this race.

The entry fee is ± $1750.00 U.S. and the musher must have previously completed a qualifying race of no less than 500 miles, or two approved races totalling 500 miles. The race crosses Alaska where the temperatures normally range from +50°F to -50°F .

The prize for the winner is around $50,000.00 U.S., plus a ½ ton GMC truck. Other prizes are given during the race (e.g. the first team to the mid-point) and prize money is given down to 20th place.

Skijoring

When Scandinavians returned from the gold rush in the west of Canada, they brought back with them the technique of hooking up sled dogs. It was natural that these early skiers combined the two interests to develop skijoring. In the United States it was more common to have horses pull skiers.

Exceptionally popular in Europe, skijoring has only begun as a sport or activity in North America. Some races (± 3 miles) and some longer events (± 30 miles a day) are now being organized in various places. Given the natural desire of most dogs to pull, a great variety of breeds of dogs (labradors, pointers, Saint Bernards, etc.) are used to haul a skier. These skis as well as the ski boots equipped with appropriate harness can be used as one would use a geepole with a sled.

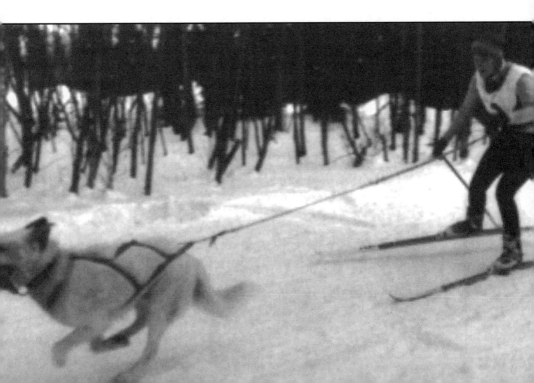

Skijoring

The Norwagian peoples developed small sleds that they called PULKAS. These small sleds were pulled by two or three dogs and the musher who is on skis, is attached to the back of this small sled. In Canada, most of the skiers are directly attached to the dogs with a wide belt. This belt is heavily padded and fitted with a quick release in case of problems. The tugline is about 8 feet long and includes a bungee to reduce shocks. Cross country skis are normally used but I think that alpine skis are easier to control. Of course, it is the easiest way to train dogs or simply to enjoy scenery; however, you have to be an experienced skier before going skijoring.

Just to imagine the speed of these dogs when you start. You will also realize that "whoa" or "stop" is a non existent concept to them, at least the first few times. Learn how to fall. Certainly it is pleasant to be able to ski with one or two of your favorite dogs. Skijoring also gives the musher an important opportunity to address certain problems, such as dogs that suddenly refuse to run, or to introduce puppies to the pleasure of pulling. This is a very good way to train new leaders to "GEE" and "HAW" commands. This is also an excellent opportunity to introduce a youngster to this facinating world. Above all, do not deprive yourself of this sport. It costs almost nothing, and you may find the experience exhilarating !

If you want to use a pulka, they are available in a very large range of prices. In competition, the total weight (comprising the harness, load, etc.) must be ± 10 pounds for one dog, 20 pounds for two dogs, 25 pounds for three dogs, and 5 pounds extra for each additional dog. The total weight is reduced by 2 pounds for each female that is in the team. This sport is extremely

Skijoring

popular in Europe. Just as for skijoring, cross country skis (light and wider) and appropriate ski boots are all that is needed.

CLUB CANIN
DE L'ESTRIE

BEST OF BREED

Stonham Photography

Judge Betty Peterson, Rosemary Hooke
and Kimlan's Rolling Stone

Certification

Does your dog display the conformation criteria for his breed? Does he have a good gait and a good temperament? Do you have the time to groom him? If he is registered by the Canadian Kennel Club you may wish to enter him in dog shows. Judges decide if he is a fine representative of his breed.

To recognize a dog's ability such as stamina, intelligence, agility, strength, attitude toward his master and team workmanship, the CKC has a certification sled dog program.

Sled dog certificate
Total accumulation of at least 50 miles, in not less than three successfully completed races (ISDRA).

Sled dog excellent certificate
Total accumulation of at least an additional 100 miles, in not less than three successfully completed races (ISDRA).

Sled dog unlimited certificate
Total accumulation of at least an additional 300 miles, in not less than three successfully completed races (ISDRA).

All races have to be governed by the current edition of the "International Sled Dog Racing Association" (ISDRA) rules.

The term "successfully completed race" means one or more heats in which the total heat times of the team is not more than 25% greater than the total average heat time of the first three positions.

Summer activities

During the summer, your dogs can become bored, and yourself as well. Why not bring them on an outing? Since they understand 'WHOA' and return when you call them, they are also able to help to carry the load, your camping gear. Begin with one dog, held by a leash, until he understands that it isn't necessary to drag you by the arm. **Normally, a dog is able to carry a load equivalent to one third of his weight.** At the end of the summer, colder temperatures permit the use of your skijoring belt, to hitch your leaders for a bicycle ride. One dog will easily pull you, two dogs will be much faster, three or more is a form of suicide. As the temperatures drop, I hitch a bigger team to a 4 wheeler or a golf cart which the motor has been re-moved. The weight of these vehicles give me full control of a team of 12 dogs and golf carts' are real cadillacs for fall expeditions.

A huge "**on wheels rendez-vous**" is organized every fall in southwest Québec. Hundreds of mushers get together with their rigs for a 5 day wild camping weekend early in October. Even people who do not have sled dogs come with their tents or campers to introduce themself to this sport. For information tel : **1-450-373-9999** or **http/www.rocler.qc.ca/apilon/**

Education

The future of sled dogs does not depend on oldtimers, but on the second millennial youngsters. Do not try to rely on someone else to promote this legendary activity. Do your homework by initiating at least one rookie every year. First, they will help in the training of your dogs, secondly, this will perpetuate knowledge; but most important, you will share your passion with new dreamers. Suggest to schools and libraries to organize demonstrations or conferences. Invite journalists from television, radio and newspaper to visit your kennel and make reports of their experience. The Upper Peninsula (Michigan) Sled Dog Association developed an **Adopt-a-Musher** program (1-900-942-7226) **what a great idea...** your best reward will be somebody telling you that it is because of you they discovered the world of sled dogs.

Costs

It is very difficult to estimate the cost of having a sled dog team. In fact, it varies between practically nothing (three dogs and an old sled) and thousands of dollars (sixteen dogs trained for long distance racing). Finances quickly become a problem when one becomes obsessed with this sport of sled dogs. **A team of six dogs with a sled, all the harnesses, etc., actually costs a lot less than a snowmobile.** Even looking at maintenance items such as feed and veterinary care, the costs are less than those of mechanical maintenance, license plates, insurance and gasoline for an average size snowmobile. So how is one satisfied with six docile dogs who will go out for a tour occasionally? How can an amateur in the sport not consider at least one litter of pups a year? And, in addition, is it possible for a breeder to sell any or all of these puppies or even keep one or two future champions? In any case, set aside some time to work because your monetary needs

Costs

will increase according to the degree of your passion for the sport. Don't fool yourself. Even if you have partici-pated in many demonstrations, races or competitions, the sale of puppies will barely cover the costs of the litter. Don't dream in technicolor ! **Sponsors are extremely rare and will anticipate a return on their investment that you probably will not be able to guarantee.** Monies earned by good placings at compe-titions may partially cover the costs of transportation and motels, but certainly will not cover the annual costs of maintenance of the dogs. Some people manage tourist enterprises - giving dog sled rides of a few hours to several days to their clients. This activity, as others, does not have a pot of gold at the end of the rainbow. But, if you must breed many puppies for sale and win many competitions with good purses, then you are not in the activity just for pleasure, but as a means of earning a living. I do not have advice to give you. I am too enamoured with the activity to be objective. I would, however, encourage you to clearly define your objec-tives and then evaluate the consequences of these objectives. Unless you wish to make a career of this activity (where many are called but few succeed), I would recommend that you choose a level of activity in the sport for which you can provide the time and money necessary to maintain. **Is it really necessary for you to be recognized by other mushers as the best in the region?** Your dogs believe you are. Isn't that what is important?

Risks

Is this sport dangerous ? In general, this activity cannot be classified as very dangerous. However, this team of half wild animals, running full speed, in wooden trails, can cause accidents. Even if your dogs are very socialized, with time and numerous occasions, chances

MISCELLANEOUS

Risks

are something can happen. Never leave a small child alone with one of your dogs. It is a risk which cannot be taken by any responsible musher. Of course, all visitors, must be advised not to intervene in any dog fights. Always take the time to show new handlers how to hold dogs (by the harness over their shoulders) and how to move them (by lifting the front legs if they pull too hard). In any accident, try to clean the wound with water, then disinfect with hydrogen peroxide. Even if your dogs have received a rabies shot, do not hesitate to see a doctor.

At the time of departure with a team, the dogs are especially excited to go. It is a must to know that the trail is clear and free from obstacles before you leave. Make sure your quick release holding the sled will release when you are ready to go. I have had mine catch and bring the just departed team to an instant standstill. This type of experience can damage sleds, dogs, musher and any passengers. When the team is negotiating a narrow serpentine forest trail or trails with obstacles, it is wise to keep the speed down. The sled may catch on a stump, hit a tree or a big rock, etc. This is not a good place to have an accident. Curiously, most sled dogs seem to speed up when the trail is difficult and dangerous.

Simon hanging onto the survival cable

If you are venturing out on unknown trails, be careful. Make sure you have detailed topographical maps and a compass (a GPS if you can afford it). Go prepared to sleep outside and above all, advise someone not going of your itinerary. In this fashion, if you do not return according to your itinerary, someone will be able to organize a search party. Avoid unknown trails on rivers, swamps and lakes. Outings on popular skidoo trails can prove to be dangerous. Each year, unfortunate encounters cause serious injuries to mushers, skidooers and sled dogs. If you hear a snowmobile while on a trail, snub your team down in an open area, and wait until the snowmobile has passed before starting out again.

Insurance

The law dictates that your animals must be under control at all times. It also makes you responsible for any damage caused by your animals. Sled dogs usually have very easy going temperaments; still, no one is immune to unforeseen situations. A broken chain results in a loose dog. The dog could bite a person, or creates a car accident or simply destroy a car seat in the vehicle where he is being kept. Normally you are obliged to have insurance coverage for civil responsibility. This will offer protection for yourself and the general public in event of an accident. Home insurance policies are usually adequate to cover the possession of two or three dogs not engaged in a commercial activity. Verify this with your insurance agent. It remains to be clarified if participation in races, dog shows, or carnivals is considered to be a commercial activity. However, **types of activities resulting in monetary gain such as tourist ventures, commercial kennels or dog rentals, will require a separate policy which takes into account the risks associated with the specific activity.**

MISCELLANEOUS

Insurance

Insurance companies usually also require a separate policy if you own an unusual number of dogs. Check with your insurance agent even if you are not involved in any commercial activity. Even if your home policy does not specifically mention dogs, the assumption will be that you have a small number of dogs. In the event of problems you may be accused of having concealed a higher than normal risk factor. Policies do not usually cover the value of your animals. This means that if one of your dogs is involved in an incident you would not be able to claim his replacement value.

I had advised my insurance agent that I owned two dozen sled dogs. **"No Problem" was the reply** ; but written confirmation was refused. Shortly after I was visited by an inspector from the company a few days after one of my females had whelped nine puppies. The result was that **I received a revocation from the company under the pretext that I surpassed normal standards.** Curiously, I was successful in obtaining the same type of coverage from another insurance broker at the same price with a $50.00 rider to cover the additional risk of this number of sled dogs. This indicated to me that my previous insurer did not understand the lack of risk of sled dogs compared to pet dogs. Don't forget to insure your equipment (buildings, trailers, sleds, etc.) for fire, theft and vandalism.

If you are organizing races, demonstrations or expeditions, you should also be insured against possible claims not only from mushers, but also from spectators. Some insurance brokers have specialized in managing dossiers involving sled dogs. Consult appropriate journals or speak with sled dog associations to find these companies.

Naya and Sierra

Blanche Neige, Blizzard and Buffy

Arctic, wheeler

Smudge, the doyen

Poppy, leader

Blizzard, leader

Claude and Anouk

CONCLUSION

It is inconceivable that a person could return from a sled dog expedition without having a profound admiration for these marvelous animals. These dogs have not yet lost the taste of adventure, the taste of discovery, the desire to excel.

Never believe that the musher's pleasure comes down to admiring the countryside, while standing behind a team of domesticated wolves. **Each minute, each second, has its share of surprises. Dixie** is distracted by a fresh trail made by a deer and I must regain her focus.... **Arctic** seems to want to pull the sled all by himself... **Blizzard** is having a good time playing with his partner **Blanche Neige... Blackwater** isn't running as usual, he will need me to put boots on him since he must have snowballs on his rear feet.... In any case, it is time to give them a short rest, **I just happen to have a caribou chop for each one ot them... They look so good, I could bite into one myself.** But I don't have time. My companions are ready to leave. They are going to be the death of me... I scarcely have time to pick up the snow hooks and I already have both feet on the brakes to limit my speed as we go down this slope...too late! I find myself in three feet of soft snow, the sled upside down; while the dogs continue to pull... **A little bit of an effort and on we go...**

Are you ready ? This may be the moment for you to **bring a dream into reality**. Don't wait any longer. This is not a question of dogs and even less one of equipment, but rather an issue of will. Take charge of this pack that awaits the one who will become the master of the team.

I won't wish for you to win the Labrador 400, but rather that you enjoy a simple trail ride at the end of the day with friends and with the dogs you love.

Anouk, leader

Anouk, Hanoré, Zamouray, Black Ice, Black Snow

Most terms which refer to dog sledding were developed in Alaska. Most words are English, but some have other derivatives. 'Musher' is believed to derive from the French 'MARCHEUR', referring to the French Canadians who drove dog teams to resupply prospectors. When it comes to commands given to dogs, it is important that you use the proper term since this offers consistency from kennel to kennel.

ALASKAN   Hybrids between huskies and other breeds to increase speed or endurance. Most of this breeding occurred up to 50 years ago.

ANALGESIC   A painkiller, such as **Aspirin®** or phenylbutazole.

BASKET   The seat in the sled, usually made of wooden slats or a sheet of plastic.

BOOTIES   Small boots which protect the feet of the dog. They are indispensable to all teams.

BRAKE   A mechanism which a musher uses to stop the sled.

BRIDLE   The equipment attached to the sled to which one connects the gangline.

LEXICON

BRUSH BOW　　A bumper. A piece of metal, wood or plastic attached to the front of the sled to help to get around obstacles.

BUNGEE　　A strong elastic cord incorporated into the lines to absorb the worst shocks and jerks.

COME GEE
HAW　　A command to the lead dogs to turn 180 degrees to the right, or to the left.

FOOT PAD　　A piece of flexible rubber installed on the runners where the musher places his feet.

GEE　　A command to the lead dogs to turn right.

HANDLE BAR　　A piece of wood arching across the back of the sled onto which the musher holds.

HANDLERS　　Helpers who handle the dogs before the start of a race or at check points.

HAW　　A command to the lead dogs to turn left.

INDIAN DOG A northern dog, mixed breed, raised in Indian villages.

LEADER A dog who directs the team from his position in front of the others is called the lead dog. Often there are two leaders directing the team. The dogs running in this position feel the responsibility of the team.

LINE OUT A command to the leaders to keep tension on the main line. This command is always used during the hook up of the team.

MALAMUTE A breed of northern dogs heavier than the Siberian Husky.

METABOLISM The chemical and physical processes within cells that produce energy for life and activity.

MUSH, HIKE
ALL RIGHT
LET'S GO A command to the team to go, to pull the sled.

MUSHER The master of the team; the driver of a dog team.

MUSHROOM The room of the musher

295

NECK LINE A cord which connects the collar of each dog to the mainline, or which connects the two lead dogs, collar to collar.

ON BY A command to continue, to overtake a team or a vehicle.

PEDALING To push the sled with one foot while
PUMPING leaving the other foot on a runner.
KICKING

QUICK RELEASE A mechanism allowing the release of the holding system when a team is ready to go.

RIGGING The complete lines including the main line and the lines for each dog, often with the sled attachments.

RUNNERS The part of the runner in contact
SHOES with the snow. Some are replaceable, sliding on a metal guide : (usually plastic).

SIBERIAN A breed, originally from Siberia,
HUSKY introduced into Alaska in 1909 by a Russian fur merchant named Goosak.

SLATS Pieces of thin wood placed on the bottom of the sled (basket).

SNOW HOOK
ICE HOOK
BRUSH HOOK A metal hook, of various shapes, used to anchor the sled during stops.

STAKE OUT LINE A chain or cable with shorter lengths connected to it to which dogs can be attached.

STAMINA Endurance, the capacity to supply sufficient effort over a long period of time (aerobic condition).

STAY A command given to a dog to stay in place, usually in a sitting position.

STOVE UP An injury, usually light, either to a dog or to a musher.

SURVIVAL
CABLE
(SNUBLINE) A line some mushers leave dragging behind the sled which they can grab if they fall, or the team begins to get away.

SWING DOGS
POINT DOGS Dogs directly behind the leaders which help leaders turn.

TEAM DOGS Dogs in the middle of the team between point dogs and wheelers are called team dogs.

TOGGLE A small piece of wood or ivory used in earlier days to attach dogs to the gangline. Now these are replaced by bronze snaps.

TOW LINE
GANGLINE The main line, connected to the sled to which all dogs are attached.

TRAIL A request made to another musher that he stop his team to let the other pass as easily as possible.

TUGLINE A line which connects the harness of each dog to the gangline. Some mushers connect their last dogs directly to the sled.

WHEEL DOGS
WHEELERS The dogs which are directly in front of the sled, the last dogs in the team. Usually these are very large dogs who are able to take the strain of hauling the sled in turns.

WHITE OUT All visibility is lost owing to blowing snow.

WHOA A musher's command to stop. Normally the musher brakes at the same time.

André Jr. Pilon, crossing the
James Bay between Ontario and Québec

bolt snap

security snap

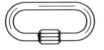

panic snap

marine quick release

quick link

wire snap

locking carabiner

swivel

METRIC CONVERSIONS

1	teaspoon	=	5 ml
1	tablespoon	=	15 ml
1	cup	=	250 ml
1	quart	=	1 litre
1	ounce (fluid)	=	30 ml
1	ounce (mass)	=	30 g
1	pound (lb)	=	454 g
1	inch	=	2,54 cm
1	foot	=	30,48 cm
1	mile	=	1,609 km
1	yard	=	91,44 cm
1	sq. ft.	=	0,092 sq.m.
1	cu. ft.	=	28,32 litres
1	pound/sq. ft.	=	0,048 Kpa

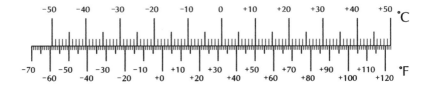

SUGGESTED READING

Magazines

DÉPART / ARRIVÉE

M. Gerry Martel
8881, rue Guy
Rawdon (Qué) Canada
J0K 1S0
Tel : (450) 882-1888

TEAM & TRAIL

P.O. Box 128
Center Harbor
New Hampshire 03226-0128
U.S.A.

TRAÎNEAU & PULKA

F.F.T.P.
Rue des Moraines
Veraz 01170 Gex, France
Tel : 89 73 37 47
Fax : 89 73 39 95

MUSH WITH PRIDE

P.O. Box 84915
Fairbanks
Alaska 99708-4915
U.S.A.

MUSHING

P.O. Box 149
Ester
Alaska 99725-0149
U.S.A.
Tel : (907) 479-0454
Mushing@polarnet.com

VET CHECK

International Sled Dog Vete-
rinary Medical Association
P.O. Box 985, Chestertown
MD 26120, U.S.A.
Tel : (410) 778-1200

Books

CARY BOB, Born to pull, Pfeifer - Hamilton Publishers, Duluth, Minnesota, 1998

COLLINS MIKI and JULIE, Dog Driver, a guide for the serious musher, Alpine Publications Inc, 1991 Loveland, CO U.S.A, ISBN : 0-931866-48-0

FIRTH JOHN, Yukon challenge, Lone Pine Publishing, Edmonton, Alberta, 1953

FLANDERS K. NOËL, The joy of running sled dogs, Alpine Publications Inc, Loveland, 1989.

HOOD H. MARY, A fan's guide to the Iditarod, Alpine Publication Inc, Loveland, 1998

KANZLER KATHLEEN, Siberian Huskies, T.F.H. Publications Inc., Neptune City, NJ07753, ISBN : 0-7938-2776-0

KAYNOR CAROL & HOE-RAITTO MARI, Skijoring, an introduction to the sport, Carol Kaynor & Mari Hoe-Raitto, Fairbanks, 1988.

LEVORSEN BELLA, Mush! A beginner's manual of sled dog training, Arner publications Inc, New York, 1992, ISBN : 0-914124-06-4

OLESEN DAVE, Cold nights fast trails, reflections of a modern dog musher, NorthWord Press Inc, Minocqua, U.S.A., 1989, ISBN : 1-55971-041-1

WELCH JIM, The speed mushing manual, How to train racing sled dogs, Sirius publishing, Eagle River, Alaska, ISBN : 0-9623643-0-4

BY THE SAME AUTHOR

This book, as well as the following publications are also available by mail :

THE 20TH CENTURY ADVENTURER - book 304 pages
A vivid description of the hunting and trapping technique experiences by the author during his many expeditions across Canada including Québec, Ontario, British Colombia, the Yukon, Magdalen Islands and Northwest Territories. This is an invitation to benefit from the diversity and abundance of Canadian Wildlife.
24.95$ (cdn)

L'UNIVERS DU CHIEN DE TRAÎNEAU - vidéo 150 min
Randonnées en vélo, en voiturette de golf, en skijoring ou sur différents types de traîneaux, sont montrées de tous les angles à travers les plus diverses activités tel que la pêche sur la glace, le piégeage des animaux à fourrure ou la simple balade dans les parcs du Québec. Un monde à découvrir. 39.95$ (cdn)

L'UNIVERS DU CHIEN DE TRAÎNEAU - Livre 304 pages
Manuel de base couvrant tous les aspects techniques de cette activité. Imaginez votre fidèle compagnon vous tirant en vélo ou en ski. Prenez les commandes d'une équipe de Huskies Sibériens pour une simple randonnée en forêt ou pour une excursion de pêche sur la glace. Indispensable pour tout amateur sérieux. 100 photos, 100 esquisses.
24.95$ (cdn)

EDITOR :
ANDRÉ PILON, 338, rue Saint-Raphaël
Valleyfield, (Québec) Canada, J6T 3A6
Tel : (450) 373-9999, Fax : (450) 373-9991
E-mail : apilon@rocler.qc.ca
Site : http/www.rocler.qc.ca/apilon/

HANDLING : 5.00$ (cdn) / per order
TAXES : as applicable